Finance
A Quantitative Introduction

Volume I

Finance
A Quantitative Introduction

Volume I

Piotr Staszkiewicz
Lucia Staszkiewicz

AMSTERDAM • BOSTON • HEIDELBERG • LONDON
NEW YORK • OXFORD • PARIS • SAN DIEGO
SAN FRANCISCO • SINGAPORE • SYDNEY • TOKYO

Academic Press is an imprint of Elsevier

Academic Press is an imprint of Elsevier
32 Jamestown Road, London NW1 7BY, UK
525 B Street, Suite 1800, San Diego, CA 92101-4495, USA
225 Wyman Street, Waltham, MA 02451, USA
The Boulevard, Langford Lane, Kidlington, Oxford OX5 1GB, UK

Notices
Knowledge and best practice in this field are constantly changing. As new research and experience broaden our understanding, changes in research methods, professional practices, or medical treatment may become necessary.

Practitioners and researchers must always rely on their own experience and knowledge in evaluating and using any information, methods, compounds, or experiments described herein. In using such information or methods they should be mindful of their own safety and the safety of others, including parties for whom they have a professional responsibility.

To the fullest extent of the law, neither the Publisher nor the authors, contributors, or editors, assume any liability for any injury and/or damage to persons or property as a matter of products liability, negligence or otherwise, or from any use or operation of any methods, products, instructions, or ideas contained in the material herein.

Library of Congress Cataloging-in-Publication Data
A catalog record for this book is available from the Library of Congress

British Library Cataloguing-in-Publication Data
A catalogue record for this book is available from the British Library

ISBN: 978-0-12-801584-1

For information on all Academic Press publications
visit our website at http://store.elsevier.com/

This book has been manufactured using Print On Demand technology. Each copy is produced to order and is limited to black ink. The online version of this book will show color figures where appropriate.

Working together
to grow libraries in
developing countries

www.elsevier.com • www.bookaid.org

DEDICATION

To Richard and Igor

TABLE OF CONTENTS

ACKNOWLEDGMENTS

We would like to express our gratitude to Prof. E. Mączyńska for her on-going support. We are indebted to the seminar participants at Institute of Corporate Finance and Investment at Warsaw School of Economics for their indications on the textbook proposal. Our students are an infinite source of motivation, and we thank you all for all your comments, remarks, and questions.

We are grateful for support at the initial stage of the project from Prof. K. Kuziak, Dr. hab. A. Adamska, and M. Bencik CSc. To Prof. M. Gruszczyński, we extend our thanks for the immediate solution on formal matters.

We are indebted to the scientific promoters of Piotr's research: Prof. M. Piotrowska for showing the life-time path and Prof. W. Ostasiewicz for crucial questions on stochastic function.

The book substantially reflects the reviews and situations we work though with our co-workers in business and government. We would like to express our thanks to Dr. K. Barborka, Dr. P. Feith, and M. Glapa as well as members of industry, CRD, and talent teams for all the business, coaching, and education experience.

We owe our gratitude to the editors: Christine Minihane, J. Scott Bentley, PhD and the Elsevier team: Mckenna Bailey, M. Murray, Anusha Sambamoorthy for their experience and professional support. We would like to thank our anonymous reviewers for valuable comments on the book prospectus. Irrespective of all the support and comments we have received, all potential errors in the text remain our responsibility.

Lucia & Piotr Staszkiewicz

INTRODUCTION

This textbook is the response to our students' needs as communicated in our performance feedback (Thanks to you all!). Initially, it was dedicated to our international students on short-term student-exchange projects. At a later stage, we learned that a textbook on an introduction to finance, written in simple English, clearly presenting the most important topics but providing examples and space for more advanced knowledge development may be a desired textbook to be used as a reference for various finance courses or as a self-study handbook for users of financial analytics.

We planned this textbook to be:

"Practically referenced soft **KISS**"

- Practical – focused on well-established high-level financial knowledge closely related to the practice.
- Referenced – the content of the textbook builds up the "backbone" for knowledge about finance or "set of bricks" that may be modified by the users for their particular needs.
- Soft – a part of the textbook is programming ready, helping users to learn and remember the solid practical and theoretical fundaments on finance.
- KISS – "keep it short and simple"; the book has been written to be concise to impart the knowledge in an understandable, short form. To meet this requirement, we imposed a page limit for each chapter.

We have introduced paragraph numbering for ease of navigation. We have left space between paragraphs to enable both students and lecturers to add their own contributions. The book is aimed at a broad audience with differing levels of knowledge of finance and different international experience. For those students with advanced pre-knowledge about finance, the textbook should provide a reference and quick overview function. For those who are starting to build their knowledge, the more advanced parts of the book may be skipped over.

Each chapter of this textbook follows the same pattern. The chapter title is followed by a mind map, which shows a synthetic picture of the chapter content and its relation in one glance. Each chapter starts with keywords relevant to the topic discussed. The interline subtitles provide navigation through the chapter structure, interspersed with examples. At the end of each chapter, there is a short summary, a set of simple self-study questions, references for further reading, and a case study with solution. The case studies are a natural extension of the main text; consolidation of prior knowledge is advised before attempting them. Revisiting the content of chapters in groups or with classmates has provided enjoyment to the majority of our students.

For a quick overview of the book content, we advise looking at the introductory mind map together with the chapter summaries. This may allow the reader to quickly digest the entire book and focus on the issues of interest in more detail.

We plan for this book to not only provide knowledge, but at the same time develop professional and academic skills and competencies such as problem-solving, analytical interpretation and building of arguments, review of documents, cross-cultural issue identification, and sensitivity or mental calculation.

This book is not intended to be a practical reference guide for financial decision-making. It presents an introduction to finance, and any professional application is not feasible with such a reduced scope and substantial theoretical assumptions. We resigned from real practice cases because in our opinion, the necessary simplification of the cases would significantly reduce their practical value. The situations and scenarios in the book are written for the purpose of this book in order to illustrate the discussed topics and to provide users with the opportunity to practice calculations and analysis.

The selection of topics discussed is based on our real-life experience. As authors, we have together more than 33 years of professional and educational experience. During our careers, we have taken sets of academic examinations and courses at Slovak, Austrian, Polish, and American Universities. Due to the international nature of our occupations and interests, we have presented deliverables in Slovak, Polish, English, and German languages and have experienced ourselves the cultural differences. We are or have been exposed to the international consulting and auditing environment, local entrepreneurs' issues, government budget verification, risk management, staff requirement assessment, and remuneration processes. We treated this mutual experience as our competitive advantage when selecting the context of this textbook. We aimed to achieve a balance between theoretical and academic content and real life relevance.

For comments on this book, please contact the authors on pstasz@shg.waw.pl.

The general structure of the book and its interconnectivity is shown in the mind map below:

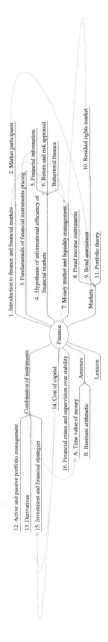

CHAPTER 1

Introduction to Finance and Financial Markets

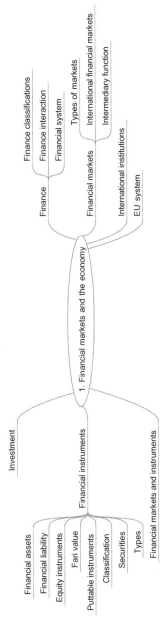

Finance: A Quantitative Introduction. http://dx.doi.org/10.1016/B978-0-12-801584-1.00001-9

1.1 FINANCE

Finance is a study of how people allocate scarce resources over time. Time is also a resource.

Finance can be divided into specific areas based on different criteria that are shown in the following table:

Subject Split	Theoretical Roots	Research Focus	Geographical Focus	Profitability
Public finance	Financial economies	Time series analysis	Local finance	Profit-oriented organization finance
Corporate finance	Financial mathematics	Financial instruments valuation	State finance	Not-for-profit organization finance
Household finance	Financial econometrics	Risk analysis	International finance	Political parties finance
	Behavioral finance		Global finance	

This book addresses the gray areas in the table for financial markets with minor elements of behavioral finance. Financial mathematics applies mainly quantitative and arithmetic tools. There are some references to other areas indicated in the table for perspective enhancement.

Corporate finance can be split in the following divisions:

- Industry finance
- Banking finance
- Insurance finance

The term corporate finance is often used to describe industry finance, whereas banking and insurance are treated separately.

The theoretical roots of finance are linked to general economic models adapted for financial issues (financial economics) or to abstract concepts applied for financial modeling (financial mathematics). They can also be used to fit actual data to a specific model type (financial econometrics). The linkage between human behavior and financial decision-making is an area of research for behavioral finance. At the same time, the financial behavior of a country is an area of interest of public finance, and the behavior of business entities falls under corporate finance. Household finance or personal finance focuses on the wealth decisions of an individual person. International finance deals with relationships between separate countries and global finance is concerned with the relationship between multinational organizations and global issues. The most developed research areas are the development of the price returns and other parameters over time (time series analysis), the value of the instrument at a given point in time (instruments valuation), and risk measurement assessment and appraisal (risk analysis). Not all organizations are profit oriented, and there are differences in financial aspects between for profit and nonprofit organizations.

1.2 INTERACTION BETWEEN FINANCE AND OTHER BRANCHES OF SCIENCE

Finance puzzle is shown in this figure.

		Mathematics			Econometrics		
				Statistics			Reporting
		Law			Accounting		Auditing
	Central banking			Finance			Book-keeping
Supervision		Macroeconomics			Microeconomics		
				Psychology			Product and market
		Sociology			Marketing		Monopoly

The gray scale represents the relative intensity of relation.

Example:

What is the link between monopoly and supervision in the context of finance?

Solution:

Some companies, for example, banks, broker dealers, and insurance companies must have a license from the supervisor in order to operate a business in major jurisdictions. This means that the market is monopolized by the state and access to it is restricted.

Financial system: the set of markets and other institutions used for financing, contracting, and the exchange of assets and risks.

1.3 PLAYERS ON MACROECONOMIC SCALE

1.3.1 Households, Companies, Government, and FX

Types of households, companies (corporate, noncorporate), governments (Democracy or other), FX – foreign entities, countries, and so on.

Example:

You take a student loan of 20,000 euros from the bank. Trace and draft the cash flow between the parties involved.

Solution:

Mr. X (surplus provided) 5000 euros, Mr. Y (surplus provided) 15,000 euros ⇒ bank (intermediate) accumulates X and Y surplus to 20,000 euros ⇒ loan (guaranteed by the state) – bank extend to me a 20,000 loan ⇒ I am the beneficiary ⇒ due to the loan received, I am able to earn more money (e.g., after studies, I get higher-paid employment); thus I have higher taxable income ⇒ I repay the loan from my higher income, plus interest, to the bank ⇒ bank returns capital to Mr. X and Mr. Y with interest (lower than earned on me) ⇒ bank has a higher income because the interest received from me is higher than paid to X and Y thus bank pays corporate income tax on it to the state ⇒ Mr. X and Y pay tax on the interest received from the bank ⇒ benefit to the state.

Note that this is a win–win position for You, Mr. X and Y, the bank, and the state, unless you make a good investment of the loan granted. Imagine that you spend that money on holidays, how would the cash flow be affected if you do not have sufficient income to repay the loan?

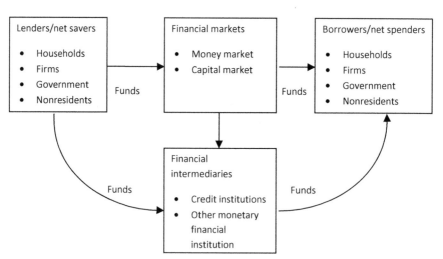

Overview of the function of the financial system.
Source: *Based on Financial Stability, ECB,* accessed on September 20, 2013.

1.4 FINANCIAL INSTRUMENTS

Investment: sacrifice of current consumption for future uncertain benefits.

Financial instrument: the most widely used definition of a financial instrument is the one used for International Financial Reporting Standards (accounting standards).

1.4.1 Financial Instrument

Financial instrument is a contract that gives rise to a financial asset of one entity and a financial liability or equity instrument of another entity.

1.4.2 Financial Asset

Financial asset is any asset that is:

- cash
- an equity instrument of another entity
- a contractual right:
  - to receive cash or other financial asset from another entity; or
  - to exchange financial assets or financial liabilities with another entity under conditions that are potentially favorable to the entity; or
- a contract that will or may be settled in the entity's own equity instruments and is:
  - a nonderivative for which the entity is or may be obliged to receive a variable number of the entity's own equity instruments
  - a derivative that will or may be settled other than by the exchange of a fixed amount of cash or another financial asset for a fixed number of the entity's own equity instruments. For this purpose, the entity's own equity instruments do not include instruments that are themselves contracts for the future receipt or delivery of the entity's own equity instruments
  - puttable instruments classified as equity or certain liabilities arising on liquidation classified by IAS 32 as equity instruments

1.4.3 Financial Liability

Financial liability is any liability that is:

- a contractual obligation:
  - to deliver cash or another financial asset to another entity; or

- o to exchange financial assets or financial liabilities with another entity under conditions that are potentially unfavorable to the entity; or
- a contract that will or may be settled in the entity's own equity instruments and is
  - o a nonderivative for which the entity is or may be obliged to deliver a variable number of the entity's own equity instruments; or
  - o a derivative that will or may be settled other than by the exchange of a fixed amount of cash or another financial asset for a fixed number of the entity's own equity instruments. For this purpose, the entity's own equity instruments do not include: instruments that are themselves contracts for the future receipt or delivery of the entity's own equity instruments; puttable instruments classified as equity; or certain liabilities arising on liquidation classified as equity instruments

1.4.4 Equity Instrument
Equity instrument is any contract that delivers a residual interest in the assets of an entity after deducting all of its liabilities.

1.4.5 Fair Value
Fair value is the amount for which an asset could be exchanged, or a liability settled, between knowledgeable, willing parties in an arm's-length transaction.

1.4.6 Puttable Instrument
Puttable instrument is a financial instrument that gives the holder the right to put the instrument back to the issuer for cash or another financial asset, or is automatically put back to the issuer on occurrence of an uncertain future event or the death or retirement of the instrument holder.

1.4.7 Long and Short
Since a financial instrument is a contract, there are two sides involved: one which is obligated (called a short position) and one which is empowered (called a long position). In accounting, the short position is close or equivalent to liability, whereas long to receivables.

The following table mentions the classification of financial instruments (financial assets or liabilities) on the basis of various parameters:

Issuer	Risk Profile	Territory	Time	Turnover	Transmission	Market Traded	Accounting*
Company	Fixed income	Local	Short time (up to 1 year)	Traded on secondary market	Transfer capital	Money	Financial assets at fair value through profit or loss
Governments	Equity	International	Medium 1–3 years	Not traded on secondary market	Transfer risk	Capital	Financial assets available for sale
Local authorities	Derivatives	Euro	Long- term; over 3 years			Derivatives	Held-to-maturity financial assets
Others		Etc				Currency	Loans and receivables
							Financial liabilities

*Accounting deals separately with financial instruments by their decomposition to asset and liabilities and records them separately. This classification is subject to changes in the IFRS standards.

1.4.8 Financial Instruments versus Securities

There is a difference between a security and a financial instrument. Not all financial instruments are securities, but all securities are financial instruments. Primarily, the securities (instruments) are designed to be traded on the secondary markets (creation of exchange). Some financial instruments can be converted into securities in a process called securitization. In the case of a bank loan, securitization allows a financial instrument to be changed from one which is not traded on the secondary market into one which is traded on the secondary market. Some instruments transfer capital (e.g., debt instruments, equity instruments), whereas other derivative instruments (e.g., credit default swaps, options) transfer solely risk. Instruments with a mixture of these characteristics are called hybrid instruments. In addition to those financial instruments that are traded on the secondary market, some instruments that are not an example of those are bank deposits or credit loans. The following table enlists the differences between the financial instruments and securities.

	Instrument	Securities
Example	Option	Share
	Forward	Bills of exchange
	CDS	Bond
	Futures	Letter of credit
Definition	Exchange of cash or cash settlement (source of definition accounting standard)	Defined in the legislation
Risk profile	Any	Identified by legal character
A detailed breakdown of the characteristics of specific instruments and securities will be provided in subsequent chapters.		

Historically, securities existed prior to the term financial instruments being introduced. Securities were the legal institution that allowed transfer of cash in return for rights and future payments or residual assets. The difference between securities and ordinary debt or liability was the possibility to create a secondary market with securities. However, from a technical point of view, each security, in order to be created, had firstly to be designed as a legal instrument, thus the risk profile was given to the public. By evolution of financial markets, the organization ruling the markets, and those involved in the over-the-counter (OTC) market, started standardizing different contracts and trading them on the secondary market. In order to capture this process, the financial accounting industry introduced the concept of a financial instrument. The result of this was that the market organizer was able to introduce to the market instruments with any kind of risk profile. The situation is more serious in the OTC and shadow markets focused on individual customers that are subject to closer and closer financial authority supervision.

Following are the different types of financial instruments:

1. Transferable securities
2. Money-market instruments
3. Units in collective investment undertakings
4. Options, futures, swaps, forward rate agreements, and any other derivative contracts relating to securities, currencies, interest rates or yields, or other derivative instruments, financial indices or financial measures which may be settled physically or in cash
5. Options, futures, swaps, forward rate agreements, and any other derivative contracts relating to commodities that must be settled in cash or may be settled in cash at the option of one of the parties (other than by reason of a default or other termination event)
6. Options, futures, swaps, and any other derivative contract relating to commodities that can be physically settled provided that they are traded on a regulated market and/or an MTF (multilateral trading facility)
7. Options, futures, swaps, forwards, and any other derivative contracts relating to commodities, that can be physically settled not otherwise mentioned in previous point and not being for commercial purposes that have the characteristics of other derivative financial instruments, having regard to whether, inter alia, they are cleared and settled through recognized clearing houses, or are subject to regular margin calls
8. Derivative instruments for the transfer of credit risk
9. Financial contracts for differences
10. Options, futures, swaps, forward rate agreements, and any other derivative contracts relating to climatic variables, freight rates, emissions allowances, inflation rates, or other official economic statistics that must be settled in cash or may be settled in cash at the option of one of the parties (other than by reason of a default or other termination event), as well as any other derivative contracts relating to assets, rights, obligations, indices, and measures not otherwise mentioned that have the characteristics of other derivative financial instruments, having regard to whether,

inter alia, they are traded on a regulated market or an MTF, are cleared and settled through recognized clearing houses, or are subject to regular margin calls

The mentioned types are used as the definition of financial instruments used for the market supervisory rules in Europe.

There is a different definition of financial instruments in accounting and financial market supervision. In essence, financial instruments are grouped into three exclusive categories on the basis of the market organization and risk profile: fixed income instruments, equity income instruments, and derivative instruments.

Category	Fixed Income Instruments	Equity Income Instruments	Derivative Instruments
Definition	Pay a specified sum of money at specified future dates	Represent the equity – assets less liabilities or the residual interest in the assets after subtracting the liabilities	Offer a return based on the return of some other underlying asset or factor (e.g., a stock price, exchange rates, interest rate)
Example	Bond Mortgage-backed securities (MBS) Assets-backed securities (ABS) Bank loans	Share	Stock option SWAP Forward

Example:

Sort the classes of financial instruments discussed above into their risk profiles.

Solution:

Fixed income	Equity	Derivatives
1 and 2	1	3–10

Note: Coverable loan that is classified as transferable securities might be classified both to equity and fixed income.

1.5 FINANCIAL MARKETS

Financial market is a place where financial transactions are executed. It can be a virtual place, for example, dotcom.

1.5.1 Structure of the Markets on the basis of the Instruments Traded

The following table mentions classification of markets on the basis of types on instruments.

Type of Markets	Money Markets	Capital Markets	Derivatives Markets	Commodity Markets	Credit-Deposits Markets	Interbank	FX Markets
Type of instruments	Interbank deposits T-bills Commercial papers Bills of exchange	Stock Bonds Investment certificates Deposit certificates	Forward Futures Options SWAPS	Non-financial instruments (raw materials)	Deposits Credits Loans	Currencies	Currencies
Major transfer	Liquidity	Capital	Risk	Asset	Liquidity details	International trade	International trade details

1.5.2 Forex and the Interbank Market

The interbank market is a market where banks and other financial institutions trade currencies. Individual retail investors cannot trade their currencies on the interbank market. Most of the transactions are performed at the banks' own risk.

The forex market is a market for currencies. It is the largest, most liquid market in the world in terms of the total cash value traded, and any entity or country may participate in this market. There is no central marketplace for currency exchange. Trade is conducted OTC. The forex market is open 24 h a day, 7 days a week and currencies are traded worldwide among the major financial centers. In the past, forex trading in the currency market had largely been the domain of large financial institutions. The advancement of the internet has altered this picture and now it is possible for less-experienced investors to buy and sell currencies through the foreign exchange platforms. The following table mentions different classifications of the financial markets.

Instance of Transaction	Level of Supervision	Type of Quotation	Type of Scale
Primary	Supervised	Continuous	Wholesale
Secondary	Non-supervised	Periodic	Details
	OTC	Mixed	

1.5.3 International Financial Market

- International bond market = Eurobond:

Eurobond is a financial instrument issued in a different currency to that of the local market. Eurobonds are sold by banks, and their secondary market is organized by the banks.

- International money market:

   Example: Company borrows short-term US dollars from London.

- International stock market:

   Example: Among others the stock exchanges of Paris, Brussels, Amsterdam, and London-based exchange – LIFFE (London International Financial Futures and Options Exchange), now trading as the Euronext.

1.5.4 Intermediary Functions of the Financial Markets

- Transfer of resources: Transfer of real economic resources from lenders to ultimate borrowers
- Enhancing income: Capital gains are income taxed and constitute revenue to the state
- Productive usage: Markets allows the issuer to undertake risky and capital-intensive projects
- Price determination: Financial markets allow for the price determination of traded financial assets
- Sale mechanism: Markets provide a mechanism for the sale of a financial asset
- Information: The activities of participants in the financial market result in the generation and subsequent dissemination of information to the various segments of the market. It thereby serves to reduce the costs of financial asset transactions

1.5.5 Financial Functions of the Financial Markets

- Providing borrowers with funds for investment
- Providing lenders with earning assets
- Providing liquidity to facilitate the trading of funds
- Providing liquidity to commercial banks
- Facilitating credit creation
- Promoting savings
- Promoting investment
- Facilitating balanced economic growth; and
- Improving trading floors

1.6 INTERNATIONAL INSTITUTIONS

- World Bank (WB) – provides long-term financing for developing countries

WB-connected institutions:

- ○ International Bank for Reconstruction and Development (IBRD) – financed with bonds issued by the WB, financing infrastructure for middle income countries (e.g., Poland)
- ○ International Development Association – grants and interest-free loans to the poorest countries (e.g., Vietnam, Bangladesh, and Nicaragua)
- International Monetary Fund (IMF) – est. 1944 – provides liquidity on the balance of payments, stabilizes exchange rates, and promotes monetary cooperation. Issues Special Drawing Rights (SDR), based on country quotas
- Bank for International Settlements (BIS) – est. 1930 – provides settlement services for national central banks. Not an issuer bank
  Note: Basel Committee focuses on systematic risk and standardizes supervisory rules. Hence, BASEL Accord (Basel is German spelling of BASLE) – it relates to the rules for the supervision of banking activities. The rules were gradually developed and extended:
- ○ 1988 – Basel Accord for credit risk – minimal capital
- ○ 1996 – Rules extended to market risk
- ○ 2006 – Basel 2 (operational risk, ICAP, disclosure rules)
- ○ 2009 – Basel 3 (buffers)

These standards are not legally binding but are recognized and applied worldwide as best practice within the industry.

1.7 INTERNATIONAL ORGANIZATION

- The International Organization of Securities Commissions (IOSCO)

The IOSCO, established in 1983, is the acknowledged international body that brings together the world's securities regulators and is recognized as the global standard setter for the securities sector. IOSCO develops, implements, and promotes adherence to internationally recognized standards for securities regulation, and works extensively with G20 countries and the Financial Stability Board (FSB) on the global regulatory reform agenda. IOSCO's membership regulates more than 95% of the world's securities markets. Its members include over 120 securities regulators and 80 other securities markets participants (i.e., stock exchanges, regional and international financial organizations). IOSCO is the only international financial regulatory organization to include all of the major emerging markets within its membership.

- The Financial Stability Board (FSB)

The FSB was established at the international level to coordinate the work of national financial authorities and international standard-setting bodies, and to develop and promote the implementation of effective regulatory, supervisory, and other financial sector policies. It brings together national authorities responsible for financial stability in significant international financial centers, international financial institutions, sector-specific international groupings of regulators and supervisors, and committees of central bank experts. Its office is located in Basel, Switzerland; it is hosted by the BIS.

International organization, for example, The World Federation of Exchanges.

1.8 EUROPEAN UNION (EU)

EU System of Financial Institutions and Regulators:
- European Systematic Risk Board (ESRB)
- European Supervisory Authorities (ESA)
  - European Banking Authority (EBA)
  - European Insurance and Occupational Pensions Authority (EIOPA)
  - European Securities and Markets Authority (ESMA)

Joint Committee is a group of representatives from the EBA, EIOPA, and ESMA.

1.9 SUMMARY

Finance is the study of the allocation of resources over time. It interrelates with a wide range of other disciplines such as law, accounting, macroeconomics, and psychology. The main players in the financial system on a macroeconomic level are households, companies, governments, and foreign participants. Investment is the sacrificing of consumption, with an expectation to achieve future uncertain gains. Financial instruments are contracts which give rise to a financial asset for one entity and a financial liability or equity instrument for another entity. The concept of financial instruments is wider than that of securities. There are numerous types of financial instruments; the most common are the fixed income instruments (bonds), residual rights (shares), and derivatives (options). Financial markets are places where transactions are executed. Nowadays, the development of the Internet has given rise to issues relating to the definition of "place." The international bond market is called Eurobond. There are many international organizations involved in financial markets, such as the WB, IMF, and BIS. The EU has developed an EU financial supervision system.

FURTHER READING

For details on financial stability, refer to European Central Bank web page (ECB n.d.). The development of the capital market and economy is presented in T. Le and T. Ooi (Le & Ooi, 2012). The costs and benefits of different levels of competition and different configurations of permissible activities in the financial sector are shown by D. Klingebiel, S. Cleasssens (Klingebiel & Cleasssens, 2001).

Y/N QUESTIONS

Number	Question	Y/N
1	A loan is a financial instrument but not a security.	Y/N
2	Cash is a financial liability.	Y/N
3	Fair value is another term for market value.	Y/N
4	A short position is equivalent to liability.	Y/N
5	A financial instrument which does not have a secondary market is a loan.	Y/N
6	A financial contract for difference is an equity instrument.	Y/N
7	MBS is an example of a fixed income instrument.	Y/N
8	The Basel Accord is a central bank for clearance settlements.	Y/N
9	EIOPA carries out supervision of ESA.	Y/N
10	SDR are issued by the IMF.	Y/N

DISCUSSIONS

1. Using the Mind Map, recall the contents of the chapter.
2. Review the EBA web page and discuss with a classmate the content of the page. Compare it with bis.org page – are there any similarities?
3. Explain the differences between a financial instrument and hazard games – for example, Black Jack.
4. Assume that a definition of financial independence is the ability to make financial decisions in the household without the

support of relatives. At what age does a child become financially independent?

5. Mark has put to the bank 3000 USD and Jasmine is taking a loan of 6000 PLN. Trace the cash flow of this transaction between the different players on the market.

SITUATION

Air crash

Two sports teams of 40 women and men travelled by plane around the world. Unfortunately, their plane crashed in the ocean. All of the players survived and reached a desert island; however, their personal belongings sank with the plane. Imagine that you are an independent observer of the shipwrecked people.

You are required to:

Construct the history of how those people created a financial market on the island. Outline the consequence of the expected processes within the group.

SOLUTION

There is no one universal scenario for the given situation. A likely one could be as follows:

The group initially will seek to satisfy the basic human needs of food, water, safety, and connection with other people. Naturally, each member of the group will possess different skills, such as farming, shooting, teaching, fishing, nursing, and so on. Those members who possess the most valuable skills for survival will be seen as more important to the micro society. Due to the interaction and developing relationships between women and men, it is rational to expect couples to have children. As a consequence, households will develop.

During the initial stage after the plane crash, the production of resources will satisfy the needs of households; however, the more specialized the households become, the more surplus production will most likely be available for exchange (e.g., a fisherman who catches fish would be able to exchange some of his fish for coconuts gathered by another group member). The initial exchange would be carried out as an exchange of one asset for another – a system known as barter, in this case fish for coconuts. However, it would be difficult to transport and exchange large quantities of fish and coconuts. Both of the products decrease in value over time, they are perishable and would begin to rot. If the fisherman has a substantial quantity of fish he would be willing to exchange some of them for coconuts and some of them for, say, medicine or clothes. Bartering would, therefore, become difficult from an organizational point of view. The new society might choose one product as a means of exchange, e.g., cigarettes. In such a system, the fisherman might exchange his surplus of fish for cigarettes and then pay for the coconuts, clothes and medicines with the cigarettes. As members of the society accumulate quantities of cigarettes in their households, theft may begin to occur. There will be motivation to establish rules and ensure that all members of the society obey them. Members of the society would have to spend time and effort maintaining the rules, which would need to be compensated for by others. Especially the cigarette holders would contribute to the organization of order and safety (e.g., by a tax contribution). Since households keep their cigarettes at home, it is likely that, in the case of a fire, those cigarettes would be lost. If one member of society becomes a treasurer (or banker) and provides a fireproof means of storage for the cigarettes, other members might deposit their cigarettes with him or her. The banker would issue a certificate as a confirmation of deposit in the bank. If they agree that the certificate would be a no-name certificate and each member who presents the certificate in front of the banker may collect the deposit of cigarettes, they start their own financial system.

Y/N QUESTIONS' ANSWERS

1	2	3	4	5	6	7	8	9	10
Y	N	N	Y	Y	N	Y	N	N	Y

CHAPTER 2

Market Participants

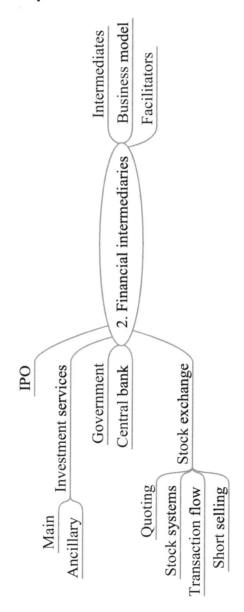

Finance: A Quantitative Introduction. http://dx.doi.org/10.1016/B978-0-12-801584-1.00002-0

2.1 FINANCIAL INTERMEDIARIES

Financial intermediaries provide customers with financial instruments that cannot efficiently be obtained by making direct transactions on security markets.

Consider:

An investment fund collects money from small investors and invests a lump sum into a security, thereby achieving a price discount due to the size of the order. This would not be achievable if a single investor were to invest directly in the same instruments.

Intermediaries are institutions that require, usually, authorization to operate in regulated financial markets. They include the following:

- Central banks
- Banks
- Investment banks
- Broker-dealers
- Mutual funds (USIT's)
- Insurance companies
- Pension and retirement funds
- Commodity dealers
- Locals
- Other institutional investors
- Non-institutional intermediaries

The previous list indicates typical organized (or legal-based) entities; however, there are number of structures based on contractual agreements such as: consortia, special purpose vehicles (used, e.g., for securitization), financial conglomerates, and joint venture schemes, which build up another layer for non-institutional intermediaries. Analysis of such a structure is beyond the scope of this book.

2.2 BUSINESS MODELS

Typical business models for the financial intermediaries are presented in the following table:

Name	Idea of Activity	Gain Earned on	Typical Customer	Basic Customer Benefit
Deposit Bank	Collects deposits at lower rates and extends the credits on higher rates. Usually there is a difference in the maturity of the credits and deposits	The difference between the rates and mismatch of maturities	Retail customer	Professional knowledge not required, product is easy but expensive
Investment Bank	Provides financing in return for financial instruments	Fees	Corporate	Lower cost of financing
Insurance Company	Accepts risk from individuals in return for a premium	Premium	Mixed	Risk transfer
Broker/Agent	Usually represents client in front of many institutions. Works on behalf of client. Brokers do act as intermediaries and do not keep inventory	Commission	Mixed	Selection costs
Dealer/Principal	Usually represents an institution in front of many clients. May buy assets on their own account and resell to clients. Dealers do keep an inventory (e.g., IPO securities, new cars)	Commission plus capital gain resulting from mismatch of time between acceptance and execution of order	Mixed	Product expertize
Mutual fund	Collects assets from clients and manages a lump sum fund	Success fee Management fee	Mixed	Acquisition of assets on gross sales (discounts available)
Asset manager	Manages a fund	Success fee Management fee	Wealthy individuals Mutual funds	Risk management
State collateral provider	Provides collateral to business to stimulate the economy. An institutional policy tool	Economic policy instrument	Business	Risk transfer
Stock exchange	Maximizes the potential turnover	Transaction costs (charge)	Only stock members (usually broker-dealers)	Credibility of the transaction
Settlement and clearing house	Matches and settles the transaction. Protects the liquidity and execution of the transaction	Transaction costs (charge)	Corporate	Evidence of transaction. Ownership is certain

Name	Idea of Activity	Gain Earned on	Typical Customer	Basic Customer Benefit
Custodian (deposits)	Provides the infrastructure for the market. Maintains the record of assets and safeguard assets	Commission	Corporate (rare retail)	Safeguards assets, limits conflict of interest
Information provider	Collect information from issuer, stock exchange, government, statistical offices and provides it to the public	Advertising fees Database access fees Tailored report fees	Mixed	Enhance information efficiency
Government	Finances the state deficit, reinvests the state surplus	Management of cost of public debts or return from investments	Corporate (rare retail)	Benchmark for market, Risk-free assets provider
Central bank	Impacts FX and interest rates via open market operation. Supervises micro requirements	Stability of prices	Corporate	Benchmark Last resort source of liquidity
Local authorities	Similar to government at local level	As government but on local level	Corporate	Low risk assets provision

2.2.1 Transaction Facilitators (TF)

A TF is not an intermediary in its purest form, but is a service provider which stimulates, facilitates, or safeguards transactions on the market. Various transaction facilitators' classes are given in the following table.

Type	Main Product	Fee Charged to	Example of a Worldwide Company
Credit ratings	Estimate the credit risk	Issuer*	Standard and Poor's
Auditor	Ensures the fairness of financial data	Ultimate owner	KPMG
Commercial lawyers	Legal compliance	Company	White and Case
Business consulting	Strategy	Company	Boston Consulting Group

*The business model of the credit ratings agencies has changed since the "Xerox" age. Prior to the self-copying (invention of the Xerox machines), the business was dedicated to investors. The main product was an independent assessment of credit risk and the formulation of the purchase or disposal of assets by the investor. Once information technology advanced, the investor buying information could relatively easily and quickly share it with other investors, thus the value of information decreased substantially over time and reduced the potential demand for credit rating agencies. In return, the agencies attracted the issuer market by extending knowledge and consulting services to include how to upgrade their issue or structure rating. This case created a natural conflict of interests and is deemed to be one of the fundamental reasons for the 2007–08 financial crisis.

2.3 INITIAL PUBLIC OFFERING (IPO)

Example:

Draw the process for the IPO and subsequent trading and withdrawal from market. Explain the role of intermediaries for industry while issuing and trading shares on the public market.

Solution:

Step	Purpose	Who	Role
Step 1	Identify an entity in need of financing	Company itself Professional advisors (auditors, tax, legal, strategic advisors), banks (investment), broker-dealers	Identify the needs, draw solution, optimize cost of financing
Step 2	Prepare the internal due diligence	Company and advisor, usually investment bank, or broker-dealer	Prepare the company for organization changes, implement reporting, internal system of control, prepare financial and quality information
Step 3	Draw the prospectus	Either investment bank or broker dealer as the leader of a consortium of advisors	Auditor – audit at least 3 years' of financial statements; legal – confirm the structure and legal status of entity; management consultants – prepare the qualitative aspects of issue, including risk assessment and prospect project management
Step 4	Draw the issue strategy	Underwriter (investment bank or broker-dealer)	Either to enter the transaction without support (direct offer to market, if not successful then no funds available), alternatively buy the entire stock and resell it – function of underwriting
Step 5	Register prospectus with the supervision authority	Broker-dealer, supervisor (e.g., SEC in USA)	Verify the compliance and completeness of the prospectus. No review of transaction risk, price, and so on
Step 6	Register the issue with repository	Custodian, depository, broker-dealer	Manage the portfolio of the owner of shares, in electronic or hard copy, depending on the system
Step 7	Road show and marketing	The leader of the consortium	Attract target investors with the proposal as outlined in the prospectus
Step 8	Investors' due diligence	Investor, financial advisor, broker-dealer	Review of prospectus and underlining data for making investment decision

Step	Purpose	Who	Role
Step 9	Establish the offer price	All involved	Different methods of establishing price including book building
Step 10	Offer stock in the primary market	Investors, settlement provider, stock exchange, clearance bank or institutions	Depending on the model used, the first offer can be performed by the supervised market or the private placement. The investors (detailed and institutional, such as pension funds) place their orders for the issue with prices
Step 11	Allocate the issue to investors	Broker-dealer, deposit (custodian), settlement provider, company	Collect payments from investors, ascertain the stock to investors, transfer the capital to the issuer (company)
Step 12	Select stock exchange for trading	Stock exchange, stock member, broker-dealer, custodian, depository, settlement and clearing	Once sold, stock might be traded on different stock exchanges; the issuer granted the right to be floated on the stock market must obey its rules, for example, reporting and corporate governance
Step 13	First trading day	Stock exchange	Listed company begins public life (end of IPO)
Step 14	Mergers and acquisition	Advisors, broker-dealers, investments banks	
Step 15	Squeeze out	Majority shareholder	Limit the control of costs
Step 16	Own shares repurchase	Management	Defence tool against hostile acquisition, wealth management tool for shareholders
Step 17	Penny stock	Market	Risk transmission mechanism
Step 18	Delisting due to insolvency	Creditors	Safeguards the residual assets. In some cases a tool for competition war
Step 19	Delisting due to achievement of the significant (greater than 90%) control	Owner	Limit the disclosure requirements
Step 19	Delisting due to reporting	Owner	Limit the discloser requirements or redesign of the business model
Step 20	Delisting due to business liquidation	Owner	End of business

Establishing the price can be done in the following ways:

1. Advisor recommendation
2. Auction amongst potential investors
3. Book building

The market itself is usually split into the following segments:

1. Primary market – the section of the market where new instruments are sold for the first time
2. Secondary market – the section of the capital market that deals with instruments already issued in the primary market

2.4 INVESTMENT SERVICES

Investment services and activities can be split into two groups: main activities and ancillary services.

Main activities are the following:

1. Reception and transmission of orders in relation to one or more financial instruments
2. Execution of orders on behalf of clients
3. Dealing on own account
4. Portfolio management
5. Investment advice
6. Underwriting of financial instruments and/or placing of financial instruments on a firm commitment basis
7. Placing of financial instruments without a firm commitment basis
8. Operation of multilateral trading facilities

Ancillary services are the following:

1. Safekeeping and administration of financial instruments for the account of clients, including custodianship and related services such as cash/collateral management
2. Granting credits or loans to an investor to allow him/her to carry out a transaction in one or more financial instruments, where the firm granting the credit or loan is involved in the transaction
3. Advice to undertakings on capital structure, industrial strategy, and related matters and advice and services relating to mergers and the purchase of undertakings
4. Foreign exchange services where these are connected to the provision of investment services
5. Investment research and financial analysis or other forms of general recommendation relating to transactions in financial instruments
6. Services related to underwriting

7. Investment services and activities as well as ancillary services of the type included under main or ancillary services related to the underlying of the derivatives, where these are connected to the provision of investment or ancillary services

The above-mentioned activities are subject to licensing under European jurisdiction.

Raising capital – basic requirements schema contains the following:

1. Prepare prospectus
2. File to the authority
3. Obtain a decision
4. Issue on the market

Note: There is a broker-dealer monopoly for offering on regulated markets in some jurisdictions.

2.5 GOVERNMENT AND CENTRAL BANK

2.5.1 Governmental Intermediaries

- Central bank or currency board
- State special purposes guarantee agencies
- Financial Supervision Authority (e.g. FSA, KNF, SEC)

2.5.2 Central Bank or Currency Board

The central bank manages the nation's money supply, interest rates, and foreign currency exchange rate. The currency board provides the local currency at a fixed rate against a foreign currency or a basket of foreign currencies and does not influence the money supply. The general function of the central bank is to maintain the stability of the local currency, usually by means of controlling inflation.

Activity of the central bank is based upon the following:

1. Open market operation
2. Capital requirements
3. Moral suasion

The open market operation is the purchase or sale of government obligation (on the money market), thereby expanding or contracting the money supply and manipulating the short-term interest rates.

The capital requirement is an amount of money required by the supervision. This is the amount expressed in money terms to be held in equity by the licensed banks and investments companies to offset the risk accumulated on the assets and operations. The Basel Committee promotes the worldwide application of the concept. The Committee also standardizes the capital requirements calculation. The standards outline the system of direct supervision combined with the system of control (state audit) and public audit.

Moral suasion is the use of a central bank's persuasive power to influence market behavior. It is often transmitted through the personality of a bank's chairman and executive directors.

Typical characteristics of central banks are the following:

1. Independent from government
2. Scope of sector supervision
3. Geographical and logical structure
4. Type of ownership
5. Type of microeconomic supervision requirements and power
6. Type of legislation status (legislator or executive body)
7. Quality of research and policy conducted

Central banks impact the real economy mainly through the short-term nominal interest rate, which in theory at least should transmit itself into changes in the long-term real rate. Within that process there is a significant time-lag. Imagine that you return home after a winter vacation and it is cold in your room. You turn up the radiator to maximum and you go to bed, but at midnight you wake up because the temperature in your room is now 30°. The small change you made in the evening has made a huge difference by midnight. A similar situation occurs when manipulating interest rates in the economy. In contrast to that process, the values of investments and financial instruments react almost immediately to the changes in rates.

Central banks were not historically uniform in terms of their ownership structure (some are owned by other institutions, e.g., Belgium and Austria, others are owned by the state, e.g., Holland and Sweden), some central banks are in fact networks, such as the Federal Reserve or European Central Bank; Central Bank, for example, NBP, Slovak Central Bank, and Czech Central Bank.

An important characteristic is its issuing function and as a last resort to provide liquidity plus financing of government loans (if allowed).

2.5.3 Central Bank Instruments

- Open market operation (with financial instruments)
- Refinance policy
- Obligatory reserves ratio
- Other instruments

The other instruments consist of, for example, moral suasion, credit limits to the banks, branches, industries, maximum repayment periods, guarantees rules, loan-taking ability, basel capital requirements, onsite control, Supervisory Review and Evaluation Process (SREP), Internal Capital and Adequacy Assessment Process (ICAAP) recommendation, personal penalties over the board members, approval and disapproval of the board member, license guaranties to the supervisors, excessive information requests.

Consider:

What does the central bank do? Issuing non-yielding assets in exchange for interest-earning assets:

- For example, Polish złoty against the US dollars.
- What is the consequence for the balance sheet position of such a bank?
- What happens to the CB balance sheet if it makes a devaluation of the local currency, how is the central bank financed?
- Can a central bank become bankrupt?

Solution:

In general, the typical exchange for non-yielding interests (local currency) against other financial instruments makes a central bank profitable by definition. However, the application of monetary policy, exchange regime, guarantees, etc. might result in significant losses to the central bank. In practice, the central bank is usually financed and recapitalized by the entire economy. A devaluation of local currency makes the liabilities of the bank less valuable than its assets, thus the central bank in principle recognizes gains in contrast to the rest of the market players.

2.5.4 New Areas and Entities Performing Intermediaries Function

- Shadow banking
- Hypermarkets and discount shops
- Mobile and voice operators
- Internet broker-dealers, FX exchange houses
- Electricity producers and providers
- CO_2 certificates traders (not commodity but derivatives market)
- Social media (e.g., Facebook, Skype)
- Peer-to-peer loan providers

2.6 STOCK EXCHANGES

A stock exchange is a form of exchange that provides services for stockbrokers and traders to trade stocks, bonds, and other financial instruments.

The primary goal of the stock exchange is to set up the price that facilitates the turnover of the instrument.

Example:

The following offers were placed to the stock exchange for ABC plc shares:

Buy		Price	Sell	
Quantity	Cumulative Quantity		Cumulative Quantity	Quantity
1	1	105	73	20
10	11	104	53	31
22	33	103	22	11
12	45	102	10	8
5	50	101	2	2
0	50	100	0	0

The table shows the order to buy and the order to sell a specific share of company ABC plc at a given moment in time. The stock exchange establishes the optimum share price for ABC plc in order to maximize turnover. At price 101, there are 50 cumulative orders, whereas at the same price, only two orders on the sell side. The maximum turnover is achievable at price 103 where 22 sell offers are accepted by 33 buy offers. The following table represents basic types of stock exchanges.

Based on the Instruments Form	Types of Instruments
Electronic	Securities
Physical trading	Financial instruments
	Commodities

Example:

What is the type of exchange where we buy and sell and buy corn?

Solution:

Commodities

2.6.1 Legal Construction of the Stock Exchange

Stock exchange: Typical elements of definition: (a) institution, (b) fixed place and timing, and (c) standardized assets.

Consider:

If an FX broker deals with its clients on FX, does it constitute an exchange?

How to set up a stock:

1. A legal right – a license (normative act structure) is prescribed in the binding legislation.
2. A multilateral agreement between parties – self-regulated bodies (e.g., UK and USA) is a private agreement to set up on the market.

The stock exchange might be driven by orders or quotes (or hybrid). On order-driven stock, the exchange accumulates, buys and sells orders, and establishes the listing price. On the quote-driven market (dealer market), numerous dealers compete with each other by providing binding bid-ask quoting.

2.6.2 Classification of Equity Markets and Stocks

1. Primary market – an exchange or market where a financial instrument is initially issued.
2. Secondary market
   a. Main market (regulated or supervised market)
   b. Parallel market (supervised but eligible for small companies)
   c. Over the counter (OTC – private market, unsupervised transaction)
3. Third market – market set up by dealers and brokers who trade instruments that are listed on the exchange away from the exchange (called a dealer market)
4. Fourth market – Alternative Trading System (ATS) – computerized, non-traditional trading systems which are complementary to the traditional exchanges and dealer markets. ATSs do not provide data on transactions and quoting. There are two types of ATS:
   a. Electronic Communication Network (ECN): electronic facilities, which match buy or sell orders. It widely disseminates orders entered by market makers to third parties and permits the orders to be executed in whole or in part.
   b. Electronic Crossing System (ECS): an electronic system which acts as a broker to match large orders. The advantage of an ECS, beside the low commission, is its ability to execute a large block order without impacting the public quote. It is useful for highly liquid stocks.

There are minor different interpretations of the previous classification. The National Association of Securities Dealers Automated Quotation (Nasdaq) national market system has been historically described as an OTC market, even if it is now supervised.

In practice, there are following three different systems of quotation used by the stock exchange:

1. Periodic system, where the quotation is done at discrete intervals
2. Continuous system, where the quotation is ongoing

3. Mixed system, where some issues are quoted continuously and others are quoted periodically

Example:

Compare the periodic and continuous systems of quotation.

Solution:

	Continuous	Periodic (Call)
Number of transactions	Requires a substantial number of transactions	Allows for an accumulation of transactions over time
Fair price	Difficult to establish if there are little or no bids or asks	More balanced
Investor size	More appropriate for bigger and skilled investors	Easier for small investors (less price fluctuation during the trading day)
Makler function	Deliver the order to market system	Set up the quoting (specialist) Might perform the market maker function

In the case of a significant drop in prices, both sides of the stock market might suspend quotation until the market reconciles new information.

The example previously assumed that to the exchange there are orders with specific prices placed. In reality, there are different order types possible, such as following:

- Market order – an order to be executed immediately at market price
- Limit order – the client specifies the minimal transaction price
- Stop order – the order is executed immediately, but if the market price reaches a client-specified level, the transaction should be stopped
- Stop limit – a combination of a stop order and limit order, where the transaction is executed within a given price range
- On the opening – this order captures the quote at the start of the trading day
- On the close – this order captures the quote at the end of the trading day
- Discretionary order – this is an order to be executed usually within a given timeframe (e.g., a day)
- Contingent switch – this order requires the sale of one financial instrument and the simultaneous purchase of another

Because different stock exchanges provide for different types of orders, the specific procedures for establishing quotes are not exactly the same.

The turnover on the market might be organized in a physical or electronic form of the financial instruments. The electronic form is less sensitive to forging of the instruments, thus is becoming more popular.

Once a transaction is concluded on the market it should be settled, reconciled, and cleared. The procedure of settlement and reconciliation is done by the clearing house.

On the market, there are two basic streams of assets. The first is the financial instruments (or their electronic equivalent), the second is transfer of cash. To enter a transaction, the investor should have two types of accounts. In electronic systems, the financial instruments are dematerialized (they no longer have a paper form and are instead an electronic entry), thus their recording is just an electronic entry in the deposit institution.

Between the investor and stock member who is empowered to execute the transaction, there could be a chain of other broker-dealers, who do

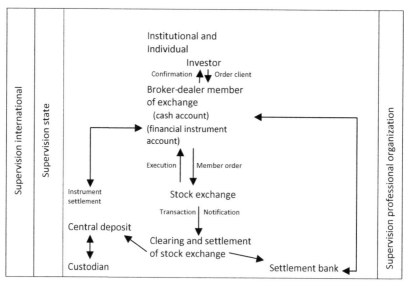

A typical flow of the transaction on the exchange and settlements

not have the status of stock member. The investor places the order with the broker-dealer. If the broker-dealer is not a stock member, the order is transferred to another broker-dealer who is a stock member. The stock member sends the order to the exchange for execution. The order is placed with the order tables, the demand and supply is matched and the transaction is executed. The stock exchange transfers the transaction details to the clearing and settlements institution. The clearance allocates net securities, quantities and debtors/creditors balances amongst either the stock members or their custodians and settlement banks depending upon the specific system. The transaction is reconciled and settled within a predefined period of time (usually 3 days).

Securities depositories or financial instruments are places where securities are kept. Nowadays instruments become dematerialized thus the depositories are kept electronically.

A typical transaction is based on a cash exchange for instruments. There is, however, a procedure to execute the transaction of the disposal of instruments, even if the investor does not possess such an instrument. This action is called short selling. The investor first borrows securities from another party, then sells them on the exchange and with the proceeds of the sale, repurchases the same quantity of securities, and repays the securities to the lender. This is feasible under the assumption that between the day of sale and the repurchase, the stock price has fallen.

Short selling is a tool which, to some extent, prevents manipulation with information and increases the liquidity of the market. One of short selling consequence is the risk of artificial assets supply. Suppose that the entire issue of the ABB shares is 1 million, but the short sell transaction is on 1.5 million shares, thus 0.5 million is an excess supply which cannot be backed up with real shares. This makes the short selling subject to numerous restrictions, both on the exchange and supervisors' level.

2.7 SUMMARY

Financial intermediaries enhance the efficiency of the market for customers. There are different types of intermediaries such as banks, investment companies, and investment funds. Each intermediary class of entities has a different business model. The models differ in terms of the activity, profit sources, typical customers, and client's major gains. Beside the intermediaries, a significant contribution to the execution of transactions is carried out by TFs.

IPO is the typical process for financing on the equity market. Investment services like portfolio management, underwriting or investments advisory are subject to licensing in some jurisdictions. Government and central banks play significant roles on the financial markets. The government is financing its deficit or investing its surplus, whereas the central bank primarily safeguards the stability of prices. There is no uniform type of exchange. The differences between stock exchanges lie within their legal organization, transaction organization, and type of instruments traded. Nowadays, electronic exchanges have become more popular. On the exchanges there are usually two basic forms of quoting: a periodic or continuous system. There are different types of order which might be placed on the broker-dealer. In an exchange transaction significant roles are played by: settlement and clearing offices, custodians, and settlement banks. The market is usually supervised by the supervision 'agency (company level) or central bank (market level). Short selling is a form of dealing without the ownership of the assets.

FURTHER READING

An overview of financial intermediation was presented by S. Greenbaum and A. Thakor (Greenbaum & Thakor, 2007) and discussion on the market structure and innovation can be found in L. Bhole (Bhole, 2004) The issues regarding the relation between central bank independence and level of inflation is discussed in A. Cukierman (Cukierman, 1992). An overview of the central banking world especially in developing regions is presented in A. Chandavarkar (Chandavarkar, 1996)

Y/N QUESTIONS

Number	Question	Y/N
1	An asset manager's primary service is for retail customers	Y/N
2	Information providers enhance the information efficiency of the market	Y/N
3	Central bank influences a short-term nominal rate	Y/N

4	An auditor is a TF	Y/N
5	Investor due diligence is executed by the IPO initiator	Y/N
6	Underwriting is an investment activity	Y/N
7	Central bank uses moral suasion to influence market behavior	Y/N
8	Mobile phone operators execute limited financial services	Y/N
9	All stock markets use the continuous quotation system	Y/N
10	A stop limit is the combination of a stop order and a market order	Y/N

DISCUSSIONS

1. Using the Mind Map recall the content of the chapter.
2. Review the EBA web page and discuss with a classmate the contents of the page. Compare it with bis.org page – are there any similarities?
3. Compare your host and home country's IPO procedure, note similarities and differences.
4. During the 2007–08 financial crisis, some European financial supervision authorities decided to suspend short selling on their stock exchanges. Discuss the impact of this on retail and investment banks.
5. Using the statistical yearbook calculate for the last 5 years the ratio of total stock capitalization (year-end) to gross domestic product (stock capitalization/GDP) for your neighbor countries. Which of the countries are more sensitive to the central bank using the stock exchange as the monetary transmission channel? Why?

SITUATION

BSSE

Bratislava Stock Exchange j.s.c. (BSSE) was founded on March 15, 1991, in conformity with a decree of the Ministry of Finance of the Slovak Republic from the year 1990. BSSE is the sole operator of a regulated market of securities in the Slovak Republic. Since June 26, 2001, BSSE has been performing its activity based on a license granted by the Financial Market Authority of the Slovak Republic. Following a decree of the National Bank of Slovakia, the license was extended to include operation of a Multilateral Trading Facility (MTF) on March 26, 2008. Trading on BSSE started on April 6, 1993.

BSSE is a joint-stock company whose activities are governed primarily by the Stock Exchange Act No. 429/2002 (Coll.), as amended by later legislation, other legal regulations and Stock Exchange Rules. BSSE is based on a membership principle which means that only Stock Exchange members, plus the National Bank of Slovakia, are authorized to directly conduct stock exchange transactions.

In the year 2000, BSSE was admitted as a corresponding member of the Federation of European Securities Exchanges (FESE). In connection with the advancing process of approximation of the capital market legislation in the Slovak Republic to the European Union's law, BSSE was admitted as associated member of the FESE in 2002. Following the Slovak Republic's entry into the European Union, BSSE has been a full member of the FESE since June 1, 2004.

You are the assistant to Mr. Walker, CFO of the New York Stock Exchange and your Board of Directors decide to make a proposal for market acquisition. Mr. Walker is now considering starting the professional due diligence but before he signs off the contract he turns to you for some advice on the Slovak Exchange System.

You are required to:

1. Identify, using Internet research, the parts of the Slovaks' financial intermediates.
2. Design a check list for the stock exchange evaluation.
3. Using www.world-exchanges.org Internet database, prepare a statistic of the number of companies listed for the period 1995–2012 on the following exchanges: Bratislava, Bucharest, Budapest, Bulgarian, Tel Aviv, Warsaw, Wiener Boerse.

SOLUTION

1. Intermediaries:
   a. Burza cenných papierov v Bratislave, a.s. (BCPB)
   b. Narodna Banka Slovenska (Slovak National Bank)
   c. Urad pre Financny Trh (FSA, now a part of the central bank)
   d. Obchodníci s cennými papiermi (broker-dealers)
   e. Banks

2. Checklist for stock evaluation (extract)

Number	Question	Yes	No	NA	Comments
1	Is the stock a separated legal entity?				
2	Is it a system of electronic exchange?				
3	Is the continuous quoting system applied?				
4	Is the stock exchange operator a public company?				
5	Is there a monopoly for the national stock exchange?				
6	Are stockbrokers allowed to trade on the floor?				
7	Is the electronic exchange IT system integrated?				
8	Is clearance a separate entity from the stock?				
9	Does the stock exchange promote financial education?				
10	Is there any arbitrage organization assigned to the stock exchange?				
...					

3. Number of listed companies on equity markets for the years 1995–2012 for selected economies.

Exchange Name	1995	1996	1997	1998	1999	2000	2001	2002	2003	2004	2005	2006	2007	2008	2009	2010	2011	2012
Bratislava SE	15	14	10	10	8	7	9	11	9	8	7	187	160	125	107	90	NA	NA
Bucharest SE	NA	NA	76	126	122	109	60	60	57	55	59	53	54	63	69	74	NA	NA
Budapest SE	42	45	48	55	66	59	NA	49	51	48	44	41	41	43	46	52	54	52
Bulgarian SE	15	9	0	18	28	23	27	351	326	332	331	347	369	404	398	390	NA	NA
Tel Aviv SE	654	655	659	662	654	665	649	624	577	578	584	606	654	642	622	613	593	549
Warsaw SE	65	83	143	198	221	225	230	202	189	216	241	265	375	458	486	585	777	867
Wiener Boerse	133	129	137	128	114	111	113	129	125	121	111	113	119	118	115	110	105	99

NA: data not available.
Source: http://www.world-exchanges.org/statistics/annual-query-tool Access date: *April 14, 2013*

Y/N QUESTIONS' ANSWERS

1	2	3	4	5	6	7	8	9	10
N	Y	Y	Y	N	Y	Y	Y	N	N

CHAPTER 3

Fundamentals of Financial Instruments Pricing

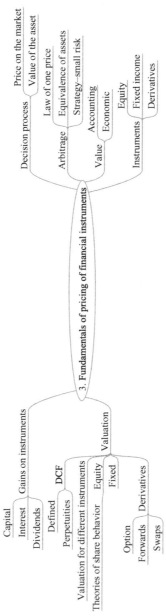

Finance: A Quantitative Introduction. http://dx.doi.org/10.1016/B978-0-12-801584-1.00003-2

3.1 DECISION-MAKING PROCESS

The financial decision-making process can be defined as:

Finding the intrinsic (fundamental) value and comparing it to the market value (or offer) and making a decision to buy (sell) or not to buy (sell).

Consequently first we need to obtain: the market value of the assets (or bid ask offers from another party). Second, we need to derive our own intrinsic view of what the price should be. The second process is the valuation of the instruments. Please note that the process itself does not define the timescale involved.

The intrinsic value or fundamental value of an asset is the price that a well-informed investor will pay for it on a competitive market. This definition requires an ideal market, which in itself is rare. In practice, there are substantial distortions to the markets. An abnormal profit is derived if the investor finds a mispriced asset on the market and thus the fundamental value is different to the market-observed price.

Example:

You are a skilled shoemaker. You make a pair of shoes which cost you 20 euros per pair including your wages. On eBay, the average price for a pair of your shoes is 40 euros. What is the fundamental value and market value of a pair of shoes?

Solution:

The market value in this case is 40 euros.

The intrinsic value is 20 euros because your wages are assumed to be your return for your work.

Note that the 20 euros' production cost is enhanced by 20 euro's profit on production. This profit is a compensation for the risk, market imperfection, and skills needed to produce the shoes (the asset). Thus, the cost value is not necessarily a good estimation of the market value with imperfect competition. However, as long as we increase the competition, the market price will approach the production costs. Thus, fundamental value assumes perfect competition.

3.2 ARBITRAGE

The intrinsic value should be unchanged for the assets on the equivalent characteristic (law of one price). Consequently two identical baskets of goods should have approximately the same price in two different shops.

Example:

Suppose a bottle costs 1 euro in a supermarket A and the same bottle costs 2 euros at supermarket B. Is this feasible?

Solution:

Suppose you buy 100 bottles at supermarket A at 100 euros and then take them to supermarket B and sell them for 200 euros. You stand to make 100 euros risk-free. Supply in shop A would be used up quickly. Seeing the demand for bottles, shop A will have a tendency to increase their price. Assuming that there are no additional costs, such as transport costs, the price will quickly be balanced between the two shops.

This process is called *arbitrage*. The law of one price is a fundamental valuation principle on the market. At two different markets the same assets have the same value (price), subject to ignoring imperfections and transaction costs.

A fundamental issue with arbitrage is that it requires the assets to be the same, but in reality even two cars made by the same producer, with the same year of production and the same model are still different, for example, in terms of parts used. Thus, the law of one is subject to numerous adjustments because of the dissimilarities in any given assets.

This problem is less visible where money is concerned. The interest rate is the cost of money, where one dollar costs the same as another one dollar. The same is true for currency exchange rates, the price of one currency (dollar) against another currency (euro) is not distinguishable because the underlying assets do not differ.

Arbitrage can be found with different notations of price such as interest rates or currency exchange rates.

Example:

Suppose that two branches of the same bank: **BI** and **BII**, offer you credit at the rate of 5% per annum at branch **BI** and 7% per annum at branch **BII**. From which branch would you take credit?

Solution:

Assuming that the transaction conditions are the same at both branches, you would take credit from branch **BI** because it is cheaper.

The law of one price also applies to exchange rates. If currencies are freely convertible, it should not matter in which currency the transaction is executed.

Example:

Suppose you would like to buy one hamburger. The price of the hamburger is 2 euros but the same hamburger in the USA costs 3 dollars. What should the exchange rate be between the euro and the dollar?

Solution:

$$2 \text{ euros} = 1 \text{ hamburger and} (=) 1 \text{ hamburger} = 3 \text{ dollars}$$

Thus:

$$2 \text{ euros} = 3 \text{ dollars} (\text{divide by } 2)$$

$$\frac{2}{2} \text{ euro} = \frac{3}{2} \text{ dollar}$$

Consequently:

$$1 \text{ euro} = 1.5 \text{ dollar}$$

Note that to set up such a relation, it is necessary to compare three "prices" having the same value (in our example dollars, euros, and hamburgers); it is thus called triangular arbitrage.

The consequence of triangular arbitrage in terms of exchange rates is that for any three currencies on an unrestricted and freely convertible market, the exchange rate between any two currencies determines the exchange rate of the third.

The execution of risk-free arbitrage is easy, does not require forecasting, and does not bear any risk. Thus, an arbitrage strategy is a safe one.

Since assets may be similar but not identical, if the value of one asset is known (e.g., from the stock exchange quoting of shares), then by comparison, the unknown value of another asset can be estimated. This process assumes that assets are sufficiently similar to be comparable.

3.3 ACCOUNTING AND ECONOMIC VALUE

Accounting valuation of assets: primary historical costs (what I paid), fair value (what I would get if I exchanged the asset with others).

Economic value of assets: present value of the future cash flows.

Example:

I get a bicycle as a present from my grandfather, but I had to pay 2 euros in delivery costs. I will use the bicycle to commute to school (a ticket costs 1 euro per day). I expect to use the bicycle for 3 years. In year 2, I expect to change the tires at a cost of 20 euros. At the end of year 4, I will scrap the bicycle for 5 euros. The cost of capital for me is 5% p.a.

Show the accounting historical value of the bicycle and its economic value.

Solution:

Accounting historical value: cost of purchase = 0 + cost of delivery = 2; the total value of the bicycle = 2 euros

Assumption: In a real-world situation, for accounting, we should not only consider cash outflow but also the value of our own work and expected future costs (guarantee claims provision, etc.).

Economic value (net present value is rounded to no decimal places).

Year	0	1	2	3	End
Initial investments–cost of delivery	(2)				
Yearly income 240 traveling days ×1 euro per ticket		240	240	240	20
Cash outflow due to tires			(20)		
Net cash flow	(2)	240	220	240	20
Discount factor	$(1+0.05)^0$ 1	$(1+0.05)^{-1}$ 0.95	$(1+0.05)^{-2}$ 0.90	$(1+0.05)^{-3}$ 0.86	$(1+0.05)^{-4}$ 0.82
Present value	(2)	228	199	207	16
Net present value	648				
Values inside parentheses indicate negative.					

The economic value is 648 euros taking into account the alternative costs of commuting to school.

Economic valuation assumptions: the expected future cash flow can be rationally predicted, the cost of capital does not change and we reinvest this at the current cost of capital rate. It is a strong simplification of reality.

Example:

Woodpecker factory S.A. published its financial statements. An extract is shown below:

Balance Sheet	31 December 2014	31 December 2013
Fixed assets	200	220
Current assets	150	140
Total assets	350	360
Equity and capital	10	50
Provisions for liabilities	120	120
Liabilities	220	190
Total liabilities	350	260

1. What is the accounting value of the Woodpecker factory S.A.?
2. What would be the intrinsic value of the company if the expected cash flow is as follows?

	2015	2016	2017	2018	Later on
Cash inflow	100	200	700	200	200
Cash outflow	(110)	(50)	(630)	(120)	(150)
Values inside parentheses indicate negative.					

and the management believes that the required rate of return should be not less than 7%?

Solution:

1. As of December 2014, accounting value is equal to 10. This is the value of equity
2.

	2015	2016	2017	2018	Later on
Cash inflow	100	200	700	200	200
Cash outflow	(110)	(50)	(630)	(120)	(150)
Net cash flow	(10)	150	70	80	50 (perpetuity)
Year	1	2	3	4	perpetuity value
Discount factor	$(1+0.07)^{-1}$	$(1+0.07)^{-2}$	$(1+0.07)^{-3}$	$(1+0.07)^{-4}$	0.07^{-1}
Perpetuity factor					14.28
Value at the 2018 of perpetuity					714.28

Discount factor value	0.934	0.873	0.816	0.762	0.762
Net cash flow multiplied by the discount factor	(9.34)	131.01	57.14	61.03	544.28
Sum	784.12				
Values inside parentheses indicate negative.					

The intrinsic value of the company is 784.1.

3.4 GROUP OF INSTRUMENTS

Basic groups of financial instruments are the following:

- Equity instrument – share (common stock) securities issued by a corporation (legal person) denominate ownership, claim for residual assets after liquidation, limited liability (the owner is only responsible for the nominal amount)
- Debt instruments – fixed income instruments. Examples: loans, credits, bills, bonds, fixed, and floating interests. Specific debt instruments: leasing, factoring, forfeiting, mortgage, and reversal mortgage
- Derivatives – financial instruments that derive their value from the price of one or more other assets such as equity, debt, foreign currencies, or commodities. Examples of derivatives: options and forward contracts, swaps, futures

The basic method for valuation of both equity and debt is discounted cash flow (DCF).

Basic Gains on Different Groups of Instruments are listed as follows:

The return from ordinary shares consists of the following:

1. Dividends
2. Capital gain (loss)

But also consider control, related party transactions, tax credits, voting rights, information access, shareholder benefits and discounts, FX differences, minority rights, squeeze out, and so on.

Fixed income instrument returns are based upon the following:

1. Interest payments and
2. Changes in the market value (realized only if sold before maturity) or
3. Redemption value less the price paid

3.5 VALUATION – DCF

Cash flow from financial instruments can be defined in time or be infinite. In its simplest form, the cash flow method follows two typical patterns:

Financial instrument: equity or debt

Defined cash flow   Perpetuity

$$Value\ of\ the\ instrument = \sum\nolimits_{t=1}^{n} \frac{C_t}{(1+r)^t}$$

$$Value\ of\ the\ instrument = \frac{annual\ payment\ (fixed)}{r}$$

where,

r = the required rate of return
n = the basis of the number of periods

3.6 EQUITY: FUNDAMENTAL ANALYSIS OF SHARE VALUES

Value of shares with an infinite cash flow expectation

Example:

I am the owner of the company that generates a cash profit of 7,000 euros per year. My cost of capital is equal to 7%. What is the value of the company to me?

Solution:

7,000/0.07 = 100,000 euros

Classification of financial markets on the basis of maturity of financial instruments is as follows:

- Money market = market for short-term debts (less than one year in duration)
- Capital market = market for long-term debts and equity securities

Market price of shares = NPV of future dividends. Model for market price of shares with constant dividend:

$$P = \frac{D}{K_e} \tag{3.1}$$

P, market price of the share ex div (excluding dividends payable); D, annual dividend per share; K_e, cost of capital (or equity, required rate of return).

Note that K_e is individual for each shareholder, thus there could be different values for any given cash flow projection.

Example:

Excon announces a yearly dividend payment of 1 USD per share for an infinite time period. What is the value of a share, if $K_e = 5\%$?

Solution:

$P = 1/0.05 = 20$ USD

Note that $P = D/K_e$ is the limit of the endless annuity of 1 at a given interest rate K_e (analytical form of the geometric series sum).

Model for constant dividend with a given growth rate:

Assuming one knows that the dividend will increase by 6% each year, then the model becomes:

$$P = D\frac{(1+g)}{K_e - g} = \frac{D_1}{K_e - g} \tag{3.2}$$

g is the growth rate, D_1 is the expected future dividend in a year. P is ex div value of share, and K_e is the cost of equity.

Example:

Iron Made Plc announces that it is going to pay 2 euro dividends, and expects this to rise at 12% each year. Assuming the cost of capital to be 8%, what is the value of the shares?

Solution:

The model is not appropriate if the growth rate is greater than the cost of capital (8–12% makes a negative value). In such a situation, another approach for valuation should be taken.

3.7 THEORIES OF SHARE PRICE BEHAVIOR

There are three following theories about share price behavior:

1. Fundamental analysis theory
2. Technical analysis (chartist theory)
3. Random walk theory

In fundamental theory, price movements are the result of changes in the intrinsic value of shares.

The everyday pricing of the stock is affected by daily fluctuations, supply and demand, liquidity, confidence, market risk-free rate, and so on. It is the basis for technical analysis performed by analysts known as chartists.

The idea behind charting is the prediction of share price movement under the assumption that the past price pattern will be repeated. There is no theoretical justification of charting.

Chartists focus on trend reversal. They base their theory on such predictions as:

1. Resistance level

The resistance and support indicates the range of the trend. If the stock price goes outside this range it indicates a change in the trend.

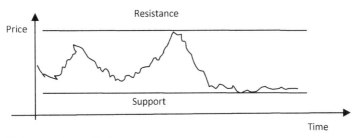

Resistance and support level

Should the price go above the resistance or below the support, the trend will be reversed.

2. Double tops and bottoms

Double tops and bottoms. If the price of a share was to grow steadily and then fall down because some investors had realized a profit, and then rose to a maximum level for the second time before starting to fall again – it would indicate a reversal of the trend.

3. "Head and shoulders" pattern

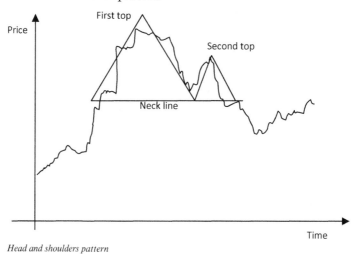

Head and shoulders pattern

A break of the neck line is an indication to sell the stock.

Chartists frequently use a moving average to determine trends.

Random walk theory is an extension of the fundamental theory – it drives the fundamental value but is subject to the behavior of investors when new information is available. Thus, the stock price is the fundamental value (intrinsic value) plus random effect.

3.8 FIXED INCOME: THE LOAN, DEBENTURES, AND LOAN STOCK VALUATION

Debentures are bonds that promise payments of interest and principals, which are not pledged on specific assets. Debentures may have a fixed or floating interest agreement. If it is a fixed irredeemable debenture, then its value is calculated as:

$$P = \frac{i}{K_d} \qquad (3.3)$$

where K_d is the required return on debentures and i is the interest (coupon rate) paid on the stock/shares.

Example:

The coupon rate amounts to 7% and the investor return 2%, what is the value of the 100 irredeemable debenture?

$P = 100 \times 0.07/0.02 = 350$

Irredeemable debentures are rare, most debentures are redeemable. For a defined cash flow, the present value method is better.

Example:

Company ABC Ltd. issues an obligation at nominal value of 100 PLN, paying 10% at par redeemable at par in 3 years. The current interest yield required by investors is 7%. What is the current market value of 200 PLN debenture?

Solution:

Year		Cash Flow	Discount 7%	
1	Interest	20	0.93	18.6
2	Interest	20	0.87	17.4
3	Interest + capital	220	0.82	180.4
				216.4

The 200 PLN debenture is worth 216.4 PLN.

Consider:

Why does the fundamental theory not hold true in practice?

Solution:

The assumptions are that: (a) all investors have the same cost of capital and (b) all investors have access to the same information on expected cash flow.

Generally, debentures can be exchanged before their maturity, so what should be the value of them?

Example:

Let us consider a situation where the holder of **ABC** Ltd. sold one obligation of the nominal value 100 **PLN** with the coupon rate of 10% p.a. fixed, in the second year, for 107 **PLN**. What would be the gain on the transaction if the return required by the market was 7%?

Solution:

1		Interest	10	0.93	9.3
2		Interest + capital	110	0.87	95.7
Total model value of the debenture					105
Paid					(107)
Result					(2)
Values inside parentheses indicate negative.					

From the position of the seller, the gain is 2, from the perspective of the buyer, the loss is 2.

The question rises what should be the cost of equity for an investor for the purchase of the instrument to be irrelevant?

The solution to the above question is an internal rate of return (**IRR**), this is the rate at which the net present value of the cash flow becomes zero. Continuing the recent example at the rate of 7%, there would be a negative value of 2, thus let us see what the **NPV** would be at the rate of 6%:

1		Interest	10	$1/1.06 = 0.94$	9.4
2		Interest + capital	110	$1/1.06^2 = 0.89$	97.9
Total					106.8
Paid					(107)
Result					(0.2)
Values inside parentheses indicate negative.					

The required **IRR** is close to 6%.

The **IRR** is a trial and error exercise.

3.9 DERIVATIVES

Derivatives are instruments that depend on the price of another asset.

3.10 OPTION

We have two parties for an option:

- Writer (Issuer): a person who issues the option
- Holder (Buyer) : a person who buys the option

We always describe the option from the perspective of the holder.

Call option: an instrument that gives its holders the right to *buy* an asset at a specified *price* on or before a specific expiration *date*.

Put option: an instrument that gives its holder the right to *sell* an asset at a specified *price* on or before a specific expiration *date*.

At issue, a writer collects an amount of money from the holder, this is called a *premium*.

The price defined in the option contract is called the strike price or the exercise price. The price observed on the stock exchange stock is the market price.

The option can be executed on any given date between the date of the contract and the expiration date (American option) or at the expiration date only (European option).

The risk profile of the option from different perspectives:

	Call	Put
Short (writer)	Very risky (infinitive)	Risky (exercise price)
Long (holder)	Risk limited to premium paid	Risk limited to premium paid

Thus, the full notation (description) of an option is given by providing the type of option and the type of side, for example, short call and long put.

	Call	Put
Short (writer)	Short call	Short put
Long (holder)	Long call	Long put

Example:

Adam is considering what amount would be payable to him if he buys a call option with an execution price of X (he takes a long call position).

1. What payoff, in terms of cash flow and gain, might he expect if the true value of the base instrument is below X, equal to X, and above X? Draw a chart.
2. How would your answer change if Adam buys a put option instead of a call option?

Solution:

1. Cash flow to Adam

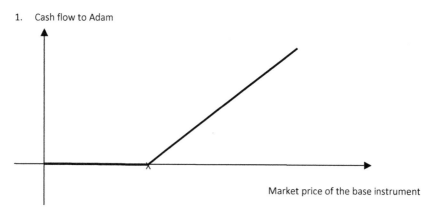

The picture above does not take into account that to buy a premium, Adam has to pay the premium to the issuer for the option, thus the gain on transaction is different to cash flow:

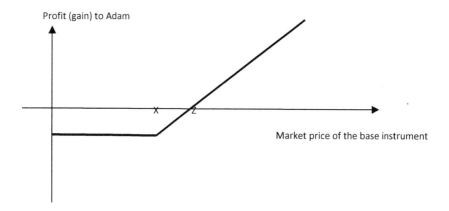

Thus, the amount $(Z - X)$ is equal to the value of the premium and transaction costs, which is equivalent to the intersection with the y-axis (profit axis).

In the case of a call option, the gain could be unlimited, while the true market price of the underlying asset goes into infinity.

Adam receives the cash flow only if the execution price is lower than the market price.

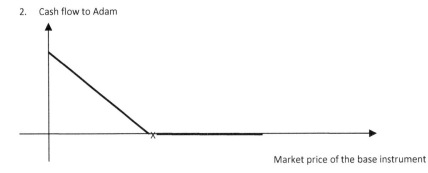

2.   Cash flow to Adam

Market price of the base instrument

Note that the maximum cash flow to Adam is equal to X if the market price is zero. And again the cash flow is different for the gain because Adam has to consider the amount of cash he has paid the issuer for the option. Thus the gain profile is as follows:

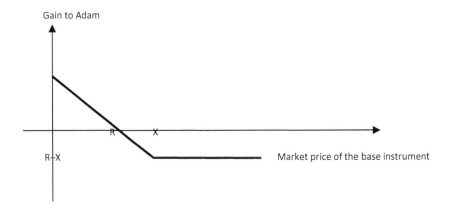

Gain to Adam

Market price of the base instrument

Note the R − X amount to the value of the premium. The space between 0 and R denotes the option in the money. If the market price of the instrument is equal to R, the option is at the money and beyond R, the option is out of the money. Sometimes, however, the descriptions of out, in, and at do not refer to the gain but the cash flow from the option meaning at the money, out of the money, and in the money option.

3.10.1 Classification of Options

Type of Market	Complexity	Instrument Issuer	Underlying Assets
Exchange trade	Vanilla	Exchange (option)	Stock
OTC	Exotic	Company (warrant)	Debt
			Index
			Other

A vanilla option is a normal call or put option that has standardized terms and no special or unusual features, whereas an exotic option is all other options which are not vanilla. The difference between an option and a warrant lies with the initiator of the instrument, which in the case of an option, the body which standardizes (set ups the rules for) the contact is the stock exchange, in the case of a warrant, the initiator is the company.

The value of an option is commonly composed of two parts:

- Forward, futures – the intrinsic value – the difference between the market value of the underlying asset and the strike price of the given option
- The time value – depends on a set of other factors which, through a multivariable, nonlinear interrelationship, reflect the discounted expected value of that difference at expiration

3.11 FORWARDS/FUTURES

A forward is a customized contract between two parties to buy or sell an asset at a specified price on a future date. A future is a contractual agreement to buy or sell a particular commodity or financial instrument at a predetermined price in the future, which is standardized by the market operator (stock exchange). The difference between a forward and future lies with the level of standardization and clearance procedures.

Both forwards and futures are symmetric contracts; this means both parties have an obligation to exercise the contract.

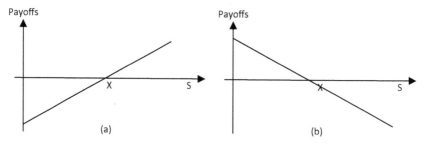

Payoffs to the (a) long position taker and (b) short position taker

where X is the exercise price (predetermined in contract) and S is the settlement (market) price.

A gain on the long side is equal to a loss on the short side.

The forwards contract may be settled with physical delivery of assets or with cash settlements.

Example:

Smith entered a contract on 15 April. As of 30 June, 10,000 shares of ABC plc must be delivered at a price of 4 euros per share.

1. Describe the difference if:
   a. Smith enters a short forward
   b. Smith enters a long futures

2. Value the contract as of 30th of April if the market price of ABC is 5 euros per share.

Solution:

1. a. If Smith enters a short forward, this means that he is obliged to deliver the 10,000 shares at the price of 4 euros. The contract is between Smith and another party (usually a bank) and is not quoted on the stock exchange. There is no need to pay any money as the guarantee for the transaction execution. If the price rises to 5 euros Smith would be reluctant to meet his obligation, thus the contra part is exposed to the risk that Smith steps away from the transaction without settlement.
   b. Smith enters a transaction and is obliged to buy the shares as of 30 June at a price of 4 euros per share. In contrary to a forward, the transaction is done through exchange via a clearing house. To set up the transaction Smith must pay in a percent of the contract value (10,000 @ 4 = 40,000 euros), known as the initial margin. The initial margin is then marked to market on a daily basis. Thus, the potential motivation of the contra parts to escape from settlement at an adverse price movement of shares is limited.

2. The contract value is 40,000 euros, the current market value is 50,000 euros thus the difference of 10,000 euros is a gain for the long position holder and a loss for the short-position holder.

With forwards/futures, the transaction is agreed on a price in the future, thus it constitutes a future market price. As a consequence, in the same moment of time, there are two types of price available on the market:

- Spot price, defined as the current price of an asset at which it can be bought/sold at a particular place and time
- Future/forward price (or sometimes forward rate), defined as the agreed upon price of an asset in a forward contract

There are different types of forwards, for example:

- Forward on interest rates called FRA – forward rate agreement
- Forward on foreign exchange currency – enabling the buying or selling of currency at a future date

3.12 SWAPS

A swap is a derivative in which two counterparties exchange cash flows of one party's financial instrument for those of the other party's financial instrument. Swaps are typically traded as OTC instruments. A swap can be viewed as the combination of two or more forwards with different exercise dates. A swap is therefore a generalization of a forward. A swap is usually a long-term contract.

A common type of swap is a "plain vanilla" interest rate swap. It is the exchange of a fixed-rate loan to a floating rate loan. A typical reason for this type of exchange is to benefit from comparative advantage. One bank may have a comparative advantage in fixed-rate markets, whereas another bank may have a comparative advantage in floating rate markets.

Example:

Bank Alfa and Bank Beta enter in to a swap contract to exchange cash flow from two underlying credits of the face value of 5 million euros. Both loans expire after 10 years and interest is paid on an annual basis. Bank Alfa receives fixed 5% p.a. on the loan, whereas Beta receives market index plus 0.2% (floating rate). What happens if the banks enter the swap?

Solution:

By entering the swap, Alfa and Beta exchange cash flows as follows:

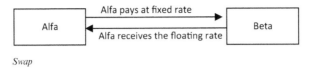

Swap

Note that this transaction is an equivalent of 10 forwards agreements on interest rates that are settled on an annual basis.

There are different kinds of swaps; following are some examples:

- Currency
- Foreign exchange
- Equity
- Interest rates
- Commodities

3.13 OTHER DERIVATIVES

The basic classes of instruments: equity, debts, options, forwards, swaps can be combined in different ways. Some examples are:

- Credit default swap (CDS) – protects lenders in the event of default on the part of the borrower by transferring the associated risk in return for periodic income payments. It is more of an option than a swap
- A future option, or option on futures – this is an option contract in which the underlying instrument is a single future contract
- Swaption – this is an option in which the buyer of the option has the right to enter into an interest rate swap (the contract of the swaption specifies whether the buyer will pay the floating rate or the fixed rate)
- Cross Currency Swap (Cross Currency Interest Rate Swap – CCIRS) – this is an agreement between two parties to exchange interest payments and principals denominated in two different currencies

3.14 SUMMARY

The value of an asset may be observed on the market or established based on a theoretical model. The price of the same asset on different markets follows the law of one price, which means that its price on both markets should have the tendency to be equal. The law of one price is a concept of an ideal market with substantial assumptions.

The economic and accounting values of an asset may differ. The most common method for asset valuation is a DCF. In order to apply a DCF, one must know the expected cash flow and cost of money (interest rate). The groups of instruments may yield perpetual cash flows or be defined in time cash flows. In the case of a perpetuity, the value of assets is the residual steady cash flow divided by the cost of financing. The value of defined in time cash flows is calculated based on the discount rate and individual installments of the cash flow.

There are a number of theories which try to explain share movement. The most typical are: fundamental analysis, chartists analysis, and random walk.

Loans and debentures usually follow a fixed cash flow pattern. The value of a derivative instrument depends on the value of other assets. An option is an asymmetric derivative whilst forwards, futures, and swaps are symmetric.

FURTHER READING

An overview of basic valuation is provided by Z. Bodie (Bodie, Merton, & Cleeton, 2012), specific discussion on financial instruments can be found in F. Fabozzi (Fabozzi, 2003), whereas there is substantial discussion of derivatives in J. Hull (Hull, 2005).

Y/N QUESTIONS

Number	Question	Y/N
1	The intrinsic value is the value observed on the market.	Y/N
2	Arbitrage relates to the fundamental value of the asset.	Y/N
3	An arbitrage strategy is usually a risky one.	Y/N
4	Swaption is an example of an equity instrument.	Y/N
5	Charting is justified with the process analysis.	Y/N
6	The writer of an option takes a long position.	Y/N
7	The most risky position in a vanilla option is a short call.	Y/N
8	Forward is a contract listed on the stock exchange.	Y/N
9	FRA is an example of a swap.	Y/N
10	CDS is a type of equity.	Y/N

DISCUSSIONS

1. Using the mind map recall the content of the chapter.
2. Explain the difference between law of one and arbitrage.
3. Identify the home and host market names of the exotic option, compare the differences.
4. Discuss what are the differences in valuation of the public listed company and limited company.
5. You agreed with the landlord, to let a flat at €400 a month payable in dollars at the month end. The rental rate is subject to revaluation if the price of hamburger (in the nearby McDonald's) changes by more than 3%. Identify the embedded option–a provision in a security that is an inseparable part of the other instrument.

SITUATION

Mr. X has created a limited liability company XFactory sp. z o.o. He expects a steady net cash flow of 10,000 PLN. Mr. X got an offer from the bank to open a risk-free deposit of 5% p.a. Assume that the risk premium for running a business is 4%.

You are required to:

1. Mr. X is approaching a professional transaction support team with the question of what are the alternatives for the valuation of his XFactory sp. z o.o? What would be the value of the business to Mr. X?
2. Describe the basic methods for the XFactory sp. z o.o.
3. State the case for and against each method.

SOLUTION

1.
$$\text{Value} = \frac{10,000}{0.05+0.04} = 111{,}111 \text{ PLN}$$

2.
   a. Cash flow (discounted net cash flow method)
   b. Accounting valuation (net equity from the accounting records)
   c. Similar companies' comparison
   d. A combination of methods a–c above.

3. State the challenges when using each of the methods:
   a. Net cash flow
      - Difficult to estimate the true cash flow from the investments.
      - The interest rate is assumed to be stable which is not true.
      - Model abstracts from the demand and supply (current request on the markets).
      - Model does not take into account non-financial rights such as voting, control, know-how, access to information.
      - It is easy to mix up the nominal cash flow with discounting based on the real interest rates.
   b. Accounting valuation
      - Accounting net equity includes non cash items like the depreciation charge, provision charges and reversal, unrealized gains and losses (e.g., foreign exchange differences).
      - Accounting is based on the past, therefore, it is not a proper indicator of the prospective future behavior of the company.
      - Accounting does not recognize intangible assets such as reputation, goodwill (except from consolidation), social capital, and so on.
   c. Comparison
      - It is difficult to find companies which are very similar. Usually companies operate in different environments with different styles, strategies, and skills of management.

Y/N QUESTIONS' ANSWERS

1	2	3	4	5	6	7	8	9	10
N	Y	N	N	N	N	Y	N	N	N

CHAPTER 4

Hypothesis of Informational Efficiency of Financial Markets

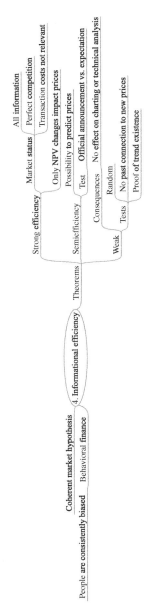

Finance: A Quantitative Introduction. http://dx.doi.org/10.1016/B978-0-12-801584-1.00004-4

4.1 EFFICIENT MARKET

An efficient capital market is when:

1. The price of securities bought and sold reflects all relevant information. Share prices change immediately to reflect new information.
2. There is competition in the market (lack of concentration) on both sides – suppliers and providers of shares.
3. Transaction costs are immaterial.

   The theorem underlying the assumption is that a market is efficient:

   If the stock market is efficient, share prices should vary in a rational way (they should vary depending on the net present values of the assets), for example:

1. When interest rates rise, investors want higher returns (assuming the same risk profile) from their investments, thus market prices of the entity will fall.
   Now, consider how the market price of a company will change if instead of the company share we deal with fixed income debentures?
2. If the company's board of directors accepts a positive NPV project then shareholders obtain the information through the stock market because the company shares will rise in anticipation of a future increase in dividends.
   Whereas, on a mature market there is an evidence that dividends are not paid. Why?
3. If the company is sued or subject to court proceedings, the shareholders will find out and so the price of its shares will fall.

Efficiency – its meaning is dependent on the context of the situation: efficiency of allocation, transaction cost efficiency, and information processing efficiency. Each meaning can be influenced by a situation of malfunctioning of the relevant financial market. In practice, the assumption of nil transaction costs is often widened to include the costs of processing information. In a perfect market, the fact of the high cost of processing information that has to be performed in order to arrive to the intrinsic value ends up with the value on the market, thus the investor is not able to gain an abnormal profit. As a consequence, there is no motivation to process all information; and therefore, the market isn't fully effective.

Transaction cost efficiency – efficiency is achieved when the broker-dealers are small and no single one can significantly influence the market.

Example:

How many broker houses operate on the Polish capital market, is the number sufficient for the market to be considered efficient?

Solution:

Approximately 55, but five of them process circa 70% of the market transactions. This indicates the weak form of the market.

Efficiency of funds allocation – funds are allocated to those entities that have higher expected NPVs. Consider the impact of state subsidies, grants, and tax credits for the investments.

Information processing efficiency – ability of the stock market to set the price of stocks and shares fairly and quickly.

Following are forms of information processing efficiency:

1. Weak form
2. Semistrong form
3. Strong form

To assess the form of the market, a test should be carried out.

4.2 WEAK FORM HYPOTHESIS

The weak form: changes in the share price are the result of new information that becomes available to investors.

The weak market does not change as a result of the anticipation of new information. The past rates of return and other historical market data do not have an impact on future rates of return; therefore, in such market, there should be no gain on trading rules based on the past rates of return.

Since information flows into the market in an unpredictable manner, its supply is unexpected and random, therefore share prices move randomly too (a random walk theory).

The weak form of the market means that the price of the shares reflects all past information – if this is the case, then technical analysis (chartist method) cannot be used at all.

The tests of the weak form are based on the following principles:

1. Share prices change randomly
2. There is no connection between the past and current share price

The types of tests are based either on statistical tests of independence between rates of returns or on comparison between results derived for the trading rules and a simple buy-and-hold strategy. To test independence, autocorrelation or the test of signs is usually applied. The tests of trading rules are more complicated due to the fact that the numbers of rules are almost unlimited.

A weak form of the market has the effect that trends in prices cannot be detected.

In order to reject the weak form of the market, it is sufficient to prove that the stock price has a trend (not stochastic, rather deterministic trend).

Example:

Consider a situation whereby a water supply company has a dividend policy:

1. To pay 5% of the profit each year; or
2. To pay 5% of the nominal value of shares each year.

How would it impact to have quoting on the market and the classification of shares and debentures on PL, GAAP, and IFRS?

Solution:

1. If the profits of the company are stable over years, a trend on the stock value can be detected, so it is contrary to the weak market hypothesis.
2. If the payment of dividends is fixed then the shares become a debenture and should be classified as liabilities instead of capital.

4.3 SEMISTRONG FORM OF EFFICIENCY

A market that has weak form and reflects all publicly available knowledge is a semistrong market.

Security prices adjust rapidly to the release of public information. An investor may gain on strategies based on information not released publically at the moment of transaction.

On a semieffective market, prices reflect all past information and all public information, thus the market is exposed to inside trading.

Players on the semistrong market are able to predict changes in prices. Their predictions can be based on time series analysis or on an examination of how quickly prices adjust to their intrinsic values after a specific significant economic event.

Exercise:

List the possible tests to detect semistrong market form.

Solution examples:

1. Expectation toward changes in interest rates announced by RPP (Council of the Monetary Policy) would impact the share price before the official announcement
2. Preparation of the M&A contract would impact both buyers' and vendors' prices

On a semiefficient market, the price should be discounted for the changes in the accounting policy of the company, so-called "windows dressing."

Problem:

Consider the impact of qualified audit opinion on the company's accounts on the company's share price. Suggest a test for the form of effectiveness of the market.

4.4 STRONG FORM OF EFFICIENCY

Share prices reflect all information available: past, public, and insider. Insider information is available to experts; therefore, they (investment managers) should outperform ordinary investors. Efficient market hypothesis (EMH) – under EMH there is no group of investors who might have access to confidential information that will allow them to achieve abnormal (above-average) profit. Thus, the test for EMH is based on a comparison of returns between different stakeholders. In an effective market, no group will be able to account for abnormal gains.

Conclusion: only changes in NPV impact share prices.

Exercise:

Explain why the units trust (mutual fund) results do not usually outperform ordinary investors.

Instead of the solution, here is a tip:

Consider the transaction costs and charges.

4.4.1 EMH: ordinary investor perspective

Ordinary investors search for a "bargain" on the market, that is, they look for undervalued shares using the following method:

$$\bar{r} = \frac{\bar{P}(1)}{P(0)} - 1 \tag{4.1}$$

where 0 denotes today, 1 is tomorrow, P is price, r is return, dash is expected.

By looking at today's price and making a prediction of the future price, the stock analyst is able to calculate the expected rate of return. The assumption made on EMH may not hold true, therefore, the best estimate of the future price $\bar{P}(1)$ is subject to errors, unexpected events, and so on. Because of the above, investors estimate how precise the $\bar{P}(1)$ is by considering the range of possible future prices – dispersion. The lower the dispersion the better is the estimate.

Based on the expected $\bar{r}$ and risk trade-off, the ordinary investor makes a decision on whether to buy, hold, or sell the stock.

The market price is the average of the sum of individual decisions weighted with their impact (size of the transaction).

The weight consists of:

1. The amount of the money invested
2. Better information on the $\bar{P}(1)$ (smaller dispersion than the rest of the market)

The ordinary shareholder's estimation of the future price of a share may be different to that of the market because:

1. He has access to different information (unlikely under EMH)
2. He is able to analyze the information differently

The chance for outperformance of the market is limited because:

1. Anyone who outperforms the market receives significant benefit – this attracts the best resources to the market;

2. The cost of entry to the analyst market is low, therefore, competition is high and analysis techniques are well developed;
3. The market is large enough to contain both forces mentioned above.

4.5 THE COHERENT MARKET HYPOTHESIS

Vaga proposed the coherent market hypothesis (CMH), stating that market prices depend on the following fundaments (intrinsic values) and crowd behavior (the behavior of a group of people):

1. Random walk (an efficient market with neutral fundaments)
2. Unstable transition (an inefficient market with neutral fundaments)
3. Coherence (crowd behavior with bullish fundaments)
4. Chaos (crowd behavior with bearish fundaments)

4.6 BEHAVIORAL FINANCE

The view taken is that there is no such thing as market information efficiency due to the fact that transactions are carried out by humans. It takes into account that humans are prone to making mistakes as a result of emotional factors. This concept is the opposite of the efficient market theories and underlines the imperfection of human behavior. It is the basis for behavioral finance.

These behavioral errors considered in behavioral finance are called biases. There are different types of bias, for example:

1. Investors tend to keep a loss position for too long or sell their profitable position too quickly
2. Growing entities are overoptimistic regarding their futures

Behavioral finance has different components such as prospect theory, cognitive errors, self-control, and risk attitude.

4.7 SUMMARY

Price reflects the information available on the market. Markets are different in their abilities to process information. There are three forms of information efficiency of the market: weak, semistrong, and strong. In weak form, the trading rules do not allow the gaining of abnormal profit, in semiweak form both trading rules and fundamental analysis are ineffective, whereas in a strong market, even inside information does not lead to extraordinary gains. If the market is efficient, there is a lack of motivation for investors to act on information; this status is unlikely in the real economy. Nevertheless, information efficiency is not always consistent with the real data, mainly due to biases of human behaviors, thus behavioral finance aims to explain these specific inconsistencies.

FURTHER READING

The proposal of market hypothesis is in the paper by E. Fama (1970), further discussion can be found in R. Shiller (1981) and J. Stiglitz (1975), J Grossman papers (Grossman & Stiglitz, 1980). Behavioral aspects of perspective D. Kahneman and A. Tversky paper (Kahneman & Tversky, 1979). A comparison of behavioral and standard finance is shown by M. Statman (1995), T. Vaga – the paper on coherent market hypothesis. Examples of efficiency testing are presented in the paper by K. Divis and P. Teply (Divis & Teply, 2005).

Y/N QUESTIONS

Number	Question	Y/N
1	The semistrong form of market reflects inside information.	Y/N
2	The weak form of market captures past information.	Y/N
3	On weak form the prices have the trend.	Y/N
4	The players on the semistrong market are able to predict prices.	Y/N
5	On weak form the changes in accounting policies are reflected in prices.	Y/N
6	The market price is an average of the individual decisions.	Y/N
7	Entry costs to the financial markets are small.	Y/N
8	The CMH states that market states depend on the fundaments and crowd behavior.	Y/N
9	Investors tend to keep too short the loss position and to sell off the profitable position too slowly.	Y/N
10	The transaction costs are assumed to be immaterial in an efficient market.	Y/N

DISCUSSIONS

1. Using the mind map, recall the contents of the chapter.
2. Compare your host and home country national exchanges; which market is more efficient. Why?
3. Design a "draft law" for the main goals of the financial market authority in respect of ad hoc information published in the market.

4. Suppose that two stock exchanges, A and B, operate in two different markets; A at semiefficient and B at weak. Consider what would happen to the market efficiency if A and B announce a merger?
5. Consider the differences in the market efficiency between the mutual exchange platform (dot com) run by a stockbroker and the main floor on the public stock exchange in terms of market information efficiency.

SITUATION

Wyborcza S.A. and Wyborowa S.A.

Wyborcza and Wyborowa are companies listed on the primary market of a stock exchange. The total number of shares issued is 9 million for Wyborcza and 24 million for Wyborowa. As of day 1, the market value of 1 share is 1 euro for Wyborcza and 8.75 euros for Wyborowa. The board of directors of Wyborowa, together with the supervisory board representative took; as of day 3, a private and classified resolution to make a takeover bid for Wyborcza for 2 euros with the aim of reducing the costs of paper and printing by 23 million euros. On day 10, Wyborowa announced an unconditional offer to purchase all the shares of Wyborowa at a price of 2 euros per share with settlement on day 20. No information on the value of savings has been disclosed. On day 15, the details on expected savings are announced.

Ignore the tax effect, accounting standards, time value of money, regulatory approvals, and any other aspects except those provided in the text.

You are required to:

1. Calculate the impact on the share prices of Wyborcza and Wyborowa for days 3, 10, and 15 for each assumption separately, on semistrong and strong forms of market.
2. Calculate the impact in exercise (a) for a cash settlement (i) and exchange of three new shares of Wyborowa for six shares of Wyborcza (ii).

SOLUTION

1. Semistrong cash offer
   a. Cash settlement

Analysts know all the past information and publicly announced current information.

Day 1

Wyborcza: 9 million shares @ 1 euro = 9 million euros value.

Wyborowa 24 million shares @ 8.75 euros = 210 million euros value.

Day 3

The private meeting does not impact the market price.

Day 10

Announced but no savings disclosed.

Wyborcza's price is raised due to the bid to 2 euros for the shares making 18 million euros value.

Wyborowa's price will move as follows:

	million euros
Opening balance value from the day 1	210
Add value of Wyborcza at day 1 prices	9
Less purchase value of Wyborcza	(18)
Net value of Wyborowa	201
Price per shares is 201 million/24 million	8.37 euros per share
Values inside parentheses indicate negative.	

The price is falling due to the fact that Wyborowa is purchasing the prospective benefits, but on a semistrong market this information is not reflected in the price.

Day 15

Announcement of savings.

Price of Wyborcza remains constant until the 20 bid is valid.

The Wyborowa price changes as follows:

The balance value from day 10 is 201 million plus savings of 23 million, divided by the number of shares 24 million, makes 9.33 per share.

Day 20

Closure of the transaction

b. Shares settlements

The prices for days 1 and 3 do not change and on day 10 the information of exchange is announced.

The value of both companies from day 1 is 219 million (210 +9). Wyborowa is going to increase its number of shares with the exchange ratio 3 for 6 times the number of Wyborcza shares. Wyborcza has 9 million shares which makes an additional issue for Wyborowa of 4.5 million shares, thus:

The combined value of the merged companies is	219 million euros
The new number of shares is 24 million plus 4.5 million	28.5 million shares
Thus the new value of the Wyborowa shares amounts to	7.68 euros per share

The value of Wyborcza reflects the same prices as Wyborowa but is adjusted for the exchange ratio this is 3/6 times 7.68 = 3.84

15 day

Announcement of savings

The value changes from 219 million to 225 (24 less 18 = 6) thus the value of share goes up to 7.89 and the value of Wyborowa, after adjustment, is 3/6 times 7.89 = 3.94.

2. Efficient market offer
   a. Cash settlement
      At day 3, all the information is available to the market thus the value of the shares is the same as on day 15 of the case above, this is Wyborowa: 9.33, Wyborcza: 2
   b. Shares settlement

In case of share settlements, the situation remains constant Wyborowa: 7.89, Wyborcza: 3.94.

Y/N QUESTIONS' ANSWERS

1	2	3	4	5	6	7	8	9	10
N	Y	N	Y	N	Y	Y	Y	N	Y

CHAPTER 5

Financial Information

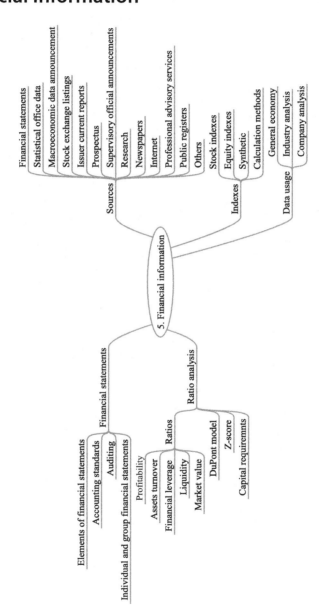

Finance: A Quantitative Introduction. http://dx.doi.org/10.1016/B978-0-12-801584-1.00005-6

5.1 SOURCES

The market transforms information into prices. There are, however, different classes and sources of information. Typical sources of financial information are the following:

1. Financial statements
2. Statistical office data
3. Macroeconomic data announcements
4. Stock exchange listings
5. Issuer current reports
6. Prospectus
7. Supervisory official announcements
8. Research
9. Newspapers
10. Internet
11. Professional advisory services
12. Public registers
13. Others (e.g., gossip, insider trading)

The information is characterized by differing levels of reliability, confidentiality, timeliness, and scope.

Example:

Sort the above sources of financial information according to their reliability, timeliness, confidentiality, and scope.

Solution:

On-Line	Reliable	Public	Detailed
Public registers (mostly)	Public registers	Public registers	
Other	Stock exchange listings	Internet	Prospectus
Stock exchange listings	Macroeconomic data announcement	Stock exchange listings	Financial statements
Internet	Statistical office data	Macroeconomic data announcement	Research/Professional advisory
Newspapers	Supervisory official announcements	Statistical offices data	Internet
Issuer current reports	Prospectus	Supervisory official announcements	Stock exchange listings
Statistical office data	Financial statements	Others	Issuer current reports
Macroeconomic data announcement	Issuer current reports	Financial statements	Supervisory official announcements

On-Line	Reliable	Public	Detailed
Financial statements	Research/Professional advisory	Issuer current reports	Statistical offices data
Research	Newspapers	Prospectus	Macroeconomic data announcement
Supervisory official announcements	Internet	Professional advisory	Public registers
Prospectus	Others		Others
Professional advisory			
With substantial delay	**Not reliable**	**Confidential**	**General**

Financial statements are reports generated by companies. They usually contain the accounting policy, balance sheet, profit and loss statement, cash flow, capital gains, funds, flows, and notes. They are usually prepared on an annual basis. These reports have a formal content, as prescribed in financial standards. There are different standards worldwide, for example, United States Generally Accepted Accounting Procedures (GAAP), United Kingdom GAAP, HB I and II, French GAAP, International Financial Reporting Standard (IFRS), PL GAAP, and so on. The financial statements are a prime source of information on the company. To ensure the quality of the information, audit procedures are carried out on the financial statements.

Statistical office data – These data differ from those in financial statements as they contain aggregated values. The structure of the data depends on the competences of the legal system and statistics offices. The data are usually presented for balance sheet items, profit and loss items, capital expenditures, industry orders, and consumption on the different levels of aggregation: local authority level, state level, global level, and so on. These data are formal in the legal sense, meaning that their provision and context are stipulated within the relevant legislation. Their reliability is determined mainly by: (i) the size of the population, (ii) organization of the statistical authorities, (iii) centralization of the technical and data processing competences. Statistical information is not subjected to audit procedures. This means that the specific singular datum of a given entity is not always audited; however, this is compensated for with the significant number of entities coming together. The frequency of the publication of the statistical data is different for different data (general economy – annually, production – quarterly, inflation – monthly). These aggregated data are treated as reliable.

Macroeconomic data – these are data gathered in a similar way to the statistics; however, they are usually interlinked with financial institutions (banks, insurance companies, etc.), relating mainly to central bank policy (reference rate and foreign exchange rates), current account data, and capital investment account plus details on settlement payments with foreign entities but also gross domestic product and unemployment figures provided by the statistical office. Macroeconomic data are usually gathered by central banks or supervisory authorities. The process is similar to that used by the statistical office; however, on the financial market, some of the data are subject to control procedures within the companies. Macroeconomic data are treated as equally reliable as statistical data.

Stock exchange data are mainly: quoting, turnover, maximum, and minimum prices of specific instruments. For some of the stock indexes, data are published, which are an important benchmark for the market. Depending on the quoting system, the data can be published at discrete intervals or close to the online. The time span between the quoting of prices is called a tick. Some strategies such as high-frequency trading rely heavily on the advantage provided when traders receive quotes to their machines more quickly than others, usually because of shorter wire distance (the distance between the broker-dealer's server and the exchange mainframe). Due to its quantity, frequency, and functional formula of achieving, stock exchange data are recognized as the basic source of financial information on a financial market.

Issuer current report – The moment a company lists its instruments, the stock exchange (or legal system) imposes information requirements. Failure to fulfill these requirements is subject to a penalties system, either public (Supervisory Authority), stipulated by the stock exchange. The data provided by the issuer differs and depends on the type of instrument, usually the more risk that is taken by the investor, the more detailed are the information requirements. In addition to this, the more public the market we look at (say from OTC to main floor), the more information should be provided. The issuer is usually obliged to provide two kinds of information, in terms of frequency (i) periodic information usually being financial statements, its forecasts or abbreviated financial statements (quarterly, semi-annually), and (ii) ad hoc information, such as information regarding significant events relevant to the company (e.g., new contracts, proceedings, receiving or losing licenses or patents, etc.).

Typically, information from the issuer is provided to the central repository monitored by the supervision authority, here the information receives a time stamp and later, the repository transmits information to the data providers (services such as Reuters, Bloomberg, etc.). Information is provided to the central repository in either paper or paperless form. In terms of electronic content, the data can be provided in an unstructured format like Word or pdf, or in a structured format like xml or xbrl. The way the data are gathered and transmitted strongly impacts the efficiency of the market and the timeliness of information provision to investors.

A *prospectus* is a set of standardized information prepared by the issuer, usually at the securities issue. A prospectus typically includes the following information:

1. Identification of the issuer
2. Identification of the type of instruments issued
3. Purpose for which the funds are being raised, including the project risk assessment, company and environmental consequences
4. Set of audited financial statements (usually for the three previous years)
5. Statements from auditors, lawyers, consultants, and management on data reliability
6. Other information required by local regulations

The prospectus is a primary information source for the IPO (Initial Public Offering).

Supervisory official announcement – The supervisory authorities for financial markets usually keep different registers which are public. They include the registers of licensed companies (banks, insurance, mutual funds, broker-dealers), issuers, transaction, obligatory disclosure (like capital requirements), aggregated data of the market, and various ad hoc reports. Besides market structure information, the supervisory authorities publicize their penalties or corrective actions taken against the market players.

Research – There are numerous scientific research studies into market behavior. Research is usually published in scientific journals where the quality of peer-reviewed papers is high. However, they are difficult for the average investor to understand, due to the technical language used. Specific and target-oriented research departments are set up with central banks and significant international intermediaries but their output has limited publicity. The research is considered to be reliable but is usually subject to significant assumptions.

Newspapers differ in the scope of financial information that they provide, and in the reliability of the information. It is almost impossible to set borders for the information provided in newspapers. A similar situation occurs with the Internet, which, when compared with newspapers, is less supervised and is a much quicker means of information distribution.

Professional advisory services are paid services. They are carried out by licensed professionals (in some countries, there is no requirement for a license). The service is a direct recommendation of what to do, tailored to the specific client based on his/her risk profile and wealth. Besides providing a service for a specific entity, the professional advisory may also provide general recommendations for the public, addressed to specific groups of investors. In the case of a conflict of interest, information should be announced publicly.

Public registers – Registers are run by the government or public organizations. They are typically cost-free and accessible through websites. Data included in the register are viewed as public, thus a contracting party cannot claim that information was unknown to it if it was disclosed in a public register. The typical register is a company house filing of corporate data, authorized auditor's register, real estate (mortgage) register, licensed entities register (like banks, insurance companies, etc.).

Data feeds are mechanisms for users to receive updated data from data sources. They are commonly used by real-time applications. Examples of financial data feed providers are Bloomberg and Reuters.

5.2 INDEXES

Stock indexes – Stock or information agencies publish indexes on the market. The indexes are usually weighted averages of the instruments' listed prices. The main purpose of the index is to provide synthetic information on the entire market. The indexes are calculated as the reference to the base date. They show the market in reference to a specific point in time.

Indexes play a significant role in financial markets. They are used as general market indicators, as an approximation of the market portfolio, and constitute the benchmark for strategy and performance appraisal.

The indexes can be split based on:

Instrument Type	Market	Calculation Methods	Number of Instruments	Weights Type	Base	Incomes Inclusion
Equity indexes	Equity market indexes	Simple average	All listed	All instruments have the same weights	Data of base	Included
Bond indexes	Money market indexes	Weighted average	Subgroups	Weights depending on price	Base value	Not included
Synthetic indexes (combination of bonds and equity)		Geometric average		Weights depending on capitalization	Base capitalization	
		Other				

Indexes may relate to a specific market like Dow Jones (equity), Barclays Capital U.S. Aggregate Bond Index (bonds) or LIBOR (money market). A currency basket used for macroeconomic policy constitutes a type of synthetic index on the currency market. The indexes are usually calculated as averages (simple, weighted or geometric) of either all instruments listed or on subgroups (e.g., construction equities index). The weight used for index construction may be based on current prices or on market capitalization. A reference point in time from which index calculations begin is called the base. The base represents the status of the market at the initiation of the index. The base can be established on value (on prices at the base date) or capitalization (market value of the portfolio at the base date).

The formal construction of the indexes:

Type	Simple Average	Average with Weights as Prices	Average with Weights as Market Values	Geometric Average
Formula	$b \frac{1}{n}\sum_{i=1}^{n}\frac{P_{it}}{P_{i0}}$	$b\frac{\sum_{i=1}^{n}P_{it}}{\sum_{i=1}^{n}P_{i0}}$	$b\frac{\sum_{i=1}^{n}n_{it}\,P_{it}}{\sum_{i=1}^{n}n_{i0}P_{i0}}$	$b\left(\frac{P_{1t}}{P_{10}}\frac{P_{2t}}{P_{20}}\ldots\frac{P_{nt}}{P_{n0}}\right)^{\frac{1}{n}}$
where:	P_{it} price of instrument i at time t, n_{it} number of instruments (e.g., total issue of shares) i at time t, and b – base (a constant).			

Example:

A recently established market operates with five components (A, B, C, D and E). On the first day of the stock exchange, the quantities of shares (millions) were as follows: A – 10, B – 5, C – 20, D – 5, E – 2. The opening quotes for shares were: A – 1, B – 3, C – 0.5, D – 2, E – 5.

Calculate the simple, arithmetic average with prices weight and market values weight as well as the geometric average indexes, if the total shares issue stays unchanged and current market prices are: A – 0.1, B – 7, C – 1, D – 3, E – 3. Assume that the base is equal to 1,000.

Solution:

Simple Average	Average with Weights as Prices	Average with Weights as Market Values	Geometric Average
$b\dfrac{1}{n}\sum\limits_{i=1}^{n}\dfrac{P_{it}}{P_{i0}}$	$b\dfrac{\sum_{i=1}^{n}P_{it}}{\sum_{i=1}^{n}P_{i0}}$	$b\dfrac{\sum_{i=1}^{n}n_{it}\,P_{it}}{\sum_{i=1}^{n}n_{i0}P_{i0}}$	$b\left(\dfrac{P_{1t}}{P_{10}}\dfrac{P_{2t}}{P_{20}}\ldots\dfrac{P_{nt}}{P_{n0}}\right)^{\frac{1}{n}}$
$b\dfrac{1}{5}\left(\dfrac{0.1}{1}+\dfrac{7}{3}+\dfrac{1}{0.5}+\dfrac{3}{2}+\dfrac{3}{5}\right)$	$b\dfrac{(0.1+7+1+3+23)}{(1+3+0.5+2+5)}$	$b\dfrac{(10\times0.1+5\times7+20\times1+5\times3+2\times3)}{(10\times1+5\times3+20\times0.5+5\times2+2\times5)}$	$b\left(\dfrac{0.1}{1}+\dfrac{7}{3}+\dfrac{1}{0.5}+\dfrac{3}{2}+\dfrac{3}{5}\right)^{\frac{1}{5}}$
If base is equal to 1,000, the indexes are as follows:			
1,306	2,965	1,400	1,455

The value of the index depends on the base and method used. It should be taken into account during the investment process.

The frequency of calculation of the indexes might be different from ongoing recalculation to periodic fixing.

Bond indexes are relatively more difficult to create to equity indexes. This is because the number of bond types is much greater than types of stocks. The bond price is affected by the duration, which changes because of maturity, coupon, and market yield. The combination of bond indexes and equity indexes is called a composite stock-bond index.

5.3 DATA USAGE

Theoretically, all data provided to the market are translated (based on the efficient market hypothesis) into the price. Before applying valuation techniques, investors use the data to perform an assessment of the potential cash flow from the investment and to assess his/her required rate of return, which actually represents the expected gain on the risk scale.

The statistical data on quoting, turnover, issues, and indexes are usually provided by the stock exchange and are used for time series techniques.

Note that the valuation procedures can be performed for all types of instruments. Full research is an expensive exercise in terms of cost, time, and skill. In practice, investors use decision heuristics (like charting) or simple valuation techniques.

The valuation process of the assets usually comprises following three stages:

1. Assessment of the general (or global) economy
2. Assessment of the industry or economy sector
3. Entity analysis

This process results in the establishment of an expected cash flow pattern and desired cost of money, which allows estimation of the intrinsic value of the entity. If the intrinsic value is above the market value, the assets are worth investment. That also indicates that there was, or there is, inefficiency in the market. If the market was information efficient, then an investor would make an expensive analysis of data to arrive at the same value as the market. That means that the efficiency of the market is limited by the cost of possessing and gathering information.

The classical inputs into a valuation model are the following:

1. Expected cash flow
2. Required return

Consequently, information provided to the market can be reflected in either the expected cash flow, or in the return, or in both. The cash flow has its own pattern of different streams: initial investment, dividend payments, interest payments, capital gains. The return may have a different time pattern, for example, it might be stable over time, it may increase or it may decrease. The required return is a measurement of the money price to the investor. It reflects different factors, the overall status of the economy and its level of risk-free rate, the expected pattern of inflation during the investment period and the risk premium that reflects the uncertainty of the estimation and the project itself.

5.4 GENERAL ECONOMY

The more integrated the global economy becomes, the greater will be the impact of a decision taken in one geographical region on the financial position of another. A rise in interest rates in the US bonds market enhances the required return of the investors, and decreases the value of assets in the other markets. Similarly, the global economic monetary policy can be restrictive, which results in an increase in short-term interest rates, the working capital becomes expensive thus the value of projects decreases due to an increase in the real long-term interest rates. On the other hand, the increase in global or national government spending impacts demand in the short-term. The economy either produces more or it runs the risk of inflation. On the other hand, spending increases the expected cash inflow, while inflation increases the required rate of return. Both factors can have different magnitudes. The general status of the economy is usually reflected in the risk-free rate relevant to the specific economy.

Besides the fiscal and monetary policy, the economy is influenced by structural changes. Typical changes relate to demography, lifestyle, technology, politics, and regulation. Societies differ with the dynamics of their demography, some societies become older whilst others become younger. The aging of society calls for retirement expenses to be met, while child booms contribute to the investment required in education and nursing. Changing lifestyles, from family structures to the single professional, alter demand for products, production changes to free time utilization and call for new services. Technology impacts the quantity, price and costs of production, product supply and labor market needs. Advanced utilization of robots in manufacturing releases members of the workforce to the market. Traditional industrial occupations are replaced with service-oriented occupations. Demand for less-qualified workers falls, thus there is an increase in natural unemployment rates, and so on. Electronic money reduces the custodian and forging risks to owners and the application of internet and mobile banking reduces the need for a huge network of physical offices. The political impacts are the redistribution of taxes, incentives provided to specific groups in society (e.g., tax relief for children) and housing allowance. By enacting laws, the system impacts the feasibility of production, for example, duties on alcoholic drinks and cigarettes reduces demand for those items. Similar intervention is the result of anti-trust and anti-monopoly administration, financial supervision, drug certification, and so on. The tax and tariff system significantly impacts international turnover.

The economy and global economy impact each country and its industry. Country-specific analysis focuses mainly on the identification of the following:

1. Business cycle
2. Long-term growth structure

The economy itself can be in one of a number of different phases in the business cycle. It can be in recession, recovery, upturn, or slowdown. It can be on the track of steady, stable growth in GDP, or the opposite may be the case. Thus, for the investor, investment into an economy with a favorable growth outlook following recession is more attractive than the opposite scenario. For some companies, the individual country impact is negligible. This is due to international differentiation. Big international companies like Coca-Cola or Siemens are not particularly sensitive to their home country's business cycles.

5.5 INDUSTRY ANALYSIS

Because of the irrelevance of country-specific analysis to some companies, the stress of the research is shifted to the industry position. The industry itself can be characterized by different factors such as following:

- Demand
- Added-value chain
- Industry life cycle
- Competitive advantages, strategies
- Structure of competitors
- Industry risks
- Government impact

All of these factors will usually impact on expected cash flow projections and stability.

5.6 COMPANY ANALYSIS

A good company is not necessarily a good investment. A well-run company will probably be priced close to its intrinsic value, thus any potential gain on share investment will be smaller than an average company whose growth prospects are promising. Thus, there is a difference between the characteristics of the company itself and the shares that the company has issued.

Category	Company	Shares	Comments
Growth	Steady increase in sales and earnings	Shares yield rates of return greater than firm's required rate of return	Where firm's return is weighted average cost of capital WACC – Weighted Average Cost of Capital

Category	Company	Shares	Comments
Economic downturn resistance	Defensive companies earnings are resistant to the overall economic downturn	Defensive shares return is not declining during economic downturn	In CAPM model defensive shares are those with low betas. Discussed later on
Cyclicality dependence	Earnings and sales follow the business cycle	Changes in rate of return higher than overall market return changes	In CAPM model shares with high betas. Discussed later on
Riskiness	Speculative company – its assets incorporate high risk for gain and loss	Speculative stocks are likely to have low profitability or loss	An example of a speculative company might be IT hardware products with substantial research and development costs. The speculative shares are those of the overpriced companies.

The estimation of the companies' parameters like sales, margin, ratios, multiples, are based on the financial statements, derivative financial statements, and forecasts provided to the market.

There is a difference between financial statements and managerial accounts. The concepts of earning, profit, margin, return can be applied both to financial statements, and managerial accounts. However, financial statements are based on publicly known rules and are subject to auditor assessment, while managerial accounts comprise information generated internally for internal purposes, whose rules are not made public. We assume that analysis is performed by a body external to the company, based on the financial statements' data definitions.

5.7 FINANCIAL STATEMENTS

Financial statements are the primary source of information about a company. This is due to the following facts:

1. The statements are prepared based on the rules which are publicly announced
2. The statements are publicly available (in specific registers)
3. The statements are usually subject to audit, thus the space for altering data is limited
4. The statements are available at periodic intervals
5. Falsification of financial statements is, in numerous jurisdictions, a legal offence subject to penalties

6. Financial statements of different companies are comparable subject to the accounting policies and GAAPs.

5.8 ELEMENTS OF FINANCIAL STATMENTS

The financial statement consists of the following:

1. An introduction, together with the accounting policy
2. Statement of financial position (balance sheet)
3. Statement of recognized profit and gains (ealier profit and loss statements)
4. Movement in equity
5. Cash flow
6. Notes and additional information

There could be different headings of points 1–6, depending on the jurisdiction.

Example:

An extract of the financial statements (IFRS)

Financial statements of ABC plc, prepared for the period ended December 31, 2015

ABC plc is a public company listed on the London Stock Exchange, incorporated as of [...]

Accounting policy

[...]

Cash and cash equivalent are valued at their nominal values.

[...]

Statement of financial position of ABC plc, as of December 31, 2015:

	As of December 31, 2014	As of December 31, 2015		As of December 31, 2014	As of December 31, 2015
	000' Euro	000' Euro		000' Euro	000' Euro
Intangible assets	20	30	Shareholder capital	80	80

Fixed assets	50	70	Capital reserves	30	17
Long-term investments	30	5	Current year profit	53	52
Total not current assets	100	105	**Total equity**	163	149
Stock	10	5	Provision of liabilities	7	8
Receivables	200	195	Long-term liabilities	21	31
Other current assets	2	3	Payables	61	50
Cash and cash equivalents	1	1	Loans	60	71
Total current assets	213	204	**Total liabilities**	149	160
Total assets	313	309	**Total liabilities and equity**	312	309

Statement of profit or loss and other comprehensive income:

	For 12 months ending December 31, 2014	For 12 months ending December 31, 2015
	000' Euro	000' Euro
Revenue	221	203
Cost of sales	(130)	(121)
Gross profit	91	82
Other expenses	(15)	(11)
Profit from operations	76	71
Finance expense	(5)	(6)
Finance income	1	2
Profit before tax	72	67
Tax expense	(20)	(17)
Profit from continuing operations	52	50
Profit/(loss) on discontinued operation, net of tax	1	2
Profit	53	52
Other comprehensive income:		
Loss on property revaluation	(2)	(1)
Remeasurement of defined benefit pension schemes	(1)	4
Share of associates' other comprehensive income	5	8
Tax relating to items that will not be reclassified	(2)	(4)
Other comprehensive income for the year, net of tax	1	0
Total comprehensive income	54	59
Values inside parentheses indicate negative.		

Cash flow statement

	As of December 31, 2014	As of December 31, 2015
	000' Euro	000' Euro
Cash flows from operating activities	80	100
Investing activities	(72)	(81)
Financing activities	(8)	(21)
Net increase in cash and cash equivalents	0	(2)
Cash and cash equivalents at beginning of year	1	3
Cash and cash equivalents at end of year	1	1
Values inside parentheses indicate negative.		

[...]

Date, (–) Board Members' Sign-off

Note that total assets is equal to total liabilities and equity (313 and 309 for 2014 and 2015, respectively), profit is reported in the statement of financial position and in the statement of profit or loss and other comprehensive income. The cash and cash equivalents at the beginning and the end of the year 2015 are directly reconcilable with the statement of financial position.

The difference between current assets and noncurrent assets lies in the liquidity; the noncurrent assets have an expected useful life of more than one year. The long-term liabilities are due later than 12 months from the balance sheet date.

The financial statements are generated internally by the entity, thus are subject to approval from management. In order to present a true and fair picture of the company finances, financial statements undergo auditing. In consequence, the financial statements should be applied after allowance for the type of opinion thereon.

Each element of the financial statement has its own purpose:

Element	Practical Usage	Typical Length
1. Introduction together with accounting policy	States the policy and objective of the entity together with accounting standards	1–20 pages
2. Statement of financial position (balance sheet)	Primary source of the accounting value of assets and liabilities	1–2 pages
3. Statement of recognized profit and gains (profit and loss statements)	Allows for operation efficiency assessment and market share analysis	1–2 pages

Element	Practical Usage	Typical Length
4. Movement in equity	Provides information on distribution and utilization of capital	1–2 pages
5. Cash flow	Allows assessment of the cash position	1–2 pages
6. Notes and additional information	Primary reference source for professional assessment of company position	Could be very long, possibly more than 100 pages

5.9 ACCOUNTING STANDARDS

Financial statements can be prepared based on different accounting standards and audited based on the different auditing standards. The application of different standards to the same company financial statements may give opposing results.

The most popular accounting standards are the following:

- IFRS
- IFRS adopted by European Union
- US GAAP
- UK GAAP
- HB II (German accounting standards)
- European Union Accounting Directives

There are semantic differences in some terms because of the different accounting and tax standards used. There are many terms which are used interchangeably, for example, sales-revenue, income-gains, earnings-profit, return, amortization-depreciation, receivables-debtors, payables-creditors, equity-capital and reserves. The IFRS does not prevent the use of different terms or terminology; however, there are certain usage policies in place. An explanation of the term used should be provided within the specific accounting policy or standards relevant to the financial statements.

5.10 AUDITING

The most widely adopted auditing standard is the International Framework for Assurance Engagement issued by the International Auditing and Assurance Standards Board (IAASB) which consists of the following:

- International Standards on Auditing
- International Standards on Review Engagements

- International Standards on Assurance Engagements
- International Standards on Related Services

The audit opinion is usually a short, formal expression prepared by the auditor stating that the financial statements show a true and fair picture in all material aspects. The audit opinion relates to the entire set of financial statements. An abbreviation or extract of the opinion is often issued together with extracts of the financial statements. This is typically the case with the annual report of the company.

The following forms of opinions can be met:

1. Unqualified: the opinion which assures that subject to materiality, data are fair and true
2. Unqualified with explanatory notes – assures that subject to materiality, data are fair and true, but to understand its context, the notes should be taken into account
3. Qualified: the auditor confirms that all data, exempt from those qualified, are fair and true. For practical purposes, the qualification statements limit the usage of financial statements. Before any analysis of the qualified financial statements can be made, the user should fully understand the nature of qualification
4. Adverse: the auditor does not agree that the picture shown in the financial statements is fair and true

An opinion which is not unqualified is called a modified opinion.

Materiality is an error or omission which alerts the financial statements users' decision. Materiality is not a precisely defined term. In practice, materiality is calculated by auditors based on the financial statements. There are different rules to assess the materiality: it could be 5–10% of profit before tax, 1–1.5% of total turnover (sales), 0.1–0.5% of total assets, or 1–5% of the net equity. Besides the quantitative aspects of materiality, some rules are given as qualitative, for example, any error which impacts the change of expectation, for example, from profit to loss, is viewed to be material.

5.11 INDIVIDUAL AND GROUP FINANCIAL STATEMENTS

Accounting distinguishes between entity financial statements and group financial statements. The single entity statements represent the position of the solo company, whereas group financial statements show the statements of a set of entities as if they were a single company. A company that controls another company is called a parent company.

Example:

Explain when the following relations take place?

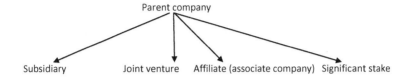

Solution:

A parent company is a company that controls another company.

A subsidiary is an entity where the parent company controls over 50%.

A joint venture is where the company is mutually controlled by at least two companies.

An affiliate or associate company is a company where the parent company has significant control (20–49%).

Significant stake is a term used for the capital requirements, where an entity controls a stake of around 5–15% of the company, which allows it to have certain corporate rights (e.g., delegate a member to the board or supervisory board).

The concept of control is approximated by the percentage stake in equity. It relates to the ability to control the operation, accounting policy, or statutory bodies.

The consolidation concept, however, fails when control is performed by a physical person.

Example:

John owns a 96% stake in Alfa Ltd and 75% in Beta Plc. Who makes the consolidated financial statements?

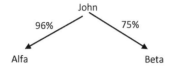

Solution:

No one. There is no financial group. Alfa and Beta are related parties, which do not constitute a financial group.

The control concepts for group accounting distinguish between direct control and indirect control. Let us consider the following situation:

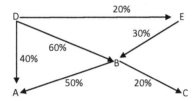

A is the subsidiary of D because D directly controls 40% of the equity of A and 60% × 50% = 30% indirectly through B, means in total 70%. D and B are the direct owners of A, whereas E is indirect.

The indirect ownership is linked to the concept of the ultimate owner.

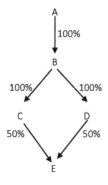

The direct owner of E is C and D, whereas the ultimate owner is A. This concept is vital for the Business Intelligence Services. The assets might be controlled by completely different entities or persons than those controlling the direct owners of the subsidiary.

Note: The physical person cannot be a parent entity. Transformation of ownership from entity to physical person results in the creation of a substantial number of related party financial structures. This process is being captured, to some extent, by the market supervision rules.

5.12 RATIO ANALYSIS

Ratio analysis is the technique usually applied to financial statements to allow for comparison of different companies.

Typical financial ratios based on financial statements:

Profitability			
	Return on sales	ROS	$\dfrac{EBIT}{Sales}$
	Return on assets	ROA	$\dfrac{EBIT}{Average\ total\ assets}$
	Return on equity	ROE	$\dfrac{Net\ profit}{Shareholders'\ equity}$
Assets turnover			
	Receivable turnover		$\dfrac{Sales}{Average\ receivable}$
	Creditors days		
	Inventory Turnover		$\dfrac{Cost\ of\ goods\ sold}{Average\ inventory}$
			$\dfrac{creditors}{Cost\ of\ goods\ sold} \times 365$
	Stock days		$\dfrac{Average\ inventory}{Cost\ of\ goods\ sold} \times 365$
	Assets Turnover		$\dfrac{Sales}{Average\ total\ assets}$
Financial leverage			
	Debt		$\dfrac{Total\ debt}{Total\ assets}$

	Time interest earned		$\dfrac{EBIT}{Interest\ expense}$
Liquidity			
	Current		$\dfrac{Current\ assets}{Current\ liabilities}$
	Working capital		Current assets less current liabilities
	Net assets		Total assets less total liabilities and provisions
	Quick (acid) test		$\dfrac{Cash + receivables}{Current\ liabilities}$
Market value			
	Price to earning		$\dfrac{Price\ per\ share}{Earning\ per\ share}$
	Market to book		$\dfrac{Price\ per\ share}{Book\ value\ per\ share}$
	Tobins Q		$\dfrac{Market\ value\ of\ assets}{Replacement\ costs}$

Note:

1. Replacement costs = original cost of assets adjusted for inflation.
2. There is theoretically an unlimited number of ratios. Their application usually requires both providing the value and the formula applied.
3. EBIT = Earning (Profit) Before Interest and Tax.

Price to earnings (P/E) and Market to book value (M/B) are often-used ratios for financial analysis.

Ratio analysis is widely applied together with an analytical review of the financial statements. There are a number of arithmetic relations between the ratios. The DuPont model allows breaking down the return on equity into three segments: profitability (measured by profit margin), operating efficiency (measured by asset turnover), and financial leverage (measured by equity multiplier). The basic formula is thus:

$$ROE = (Net\ profit/Sales) \times (Sales/Assets) \times (Assets/Equity) = (Net\ Profit/Equity)$$
$$(Profit\ margin) \times (Asset\ turnover) \times (Equity\ multiplier)$$

A combination of ratios might be used as a failure prediction tool. The idea behind this approach is to calculate one number as a combination of different ratios. The combined value (let us call it Z score) is then compared with the benchmark (cut-off value) to arrive at the conclusion if a given entity is likely to fail. The Altman Z score was historically the pioneering model and thereafter, a number of specific models have been constructed.

Example:

The model of J. Gajdki and D. Stosa is given with the following formula:

$$Z = 0.7732059 + 0.0856425X_1 + 0.0007747X_2 + 0.9220985X_3 + 0.6535995X_4 - 0.594687X_5$$

where:

X_1 = sales revenues/total assets,

X_2 = short-term payables/cost of sales,

X_3 = profit after tax/total assets,

X_4 = profit before tax/sales revenues, and

X_5 = total liabilities/total assets.

The cutoff point of the model is 0.45. Z above this value indicates a lack of default risk.

Assess whether the ABC plc, as of December 31, 2015, is at default risk?

Solution:

$$X_1 = \frac{\text{sales revenues}}{\text{total assets}} = \frac{203}{309} = 0.657$$

$$X_2 = \frac{\text{short} - \text{term payables}}{\text{cost of sales}} = \frac{160 - 31 - 8}{221} = 0.547$$

$$X_3 = \frac{\text{profit after tax}}{\text{total assets}} = \frac{52}{309} = 0.168$$

$$X_4 = \frac{\text{profit before tax}}{\text{sales revenues}} = \frac{67}{203} = 0.330$$

$$X_5 = \frac{\text{total liabilities}}{\text{total assets}} = \frac{160}{309} = 0.518$$

thus Z is equal to:

$$Z = 0.7732059 + 0.0856425 \times 0.657 + 0.0007747 \times 0.547 + 0.9220985$$
$$\times\, 0.168 + 0.6535995 \times 0.330 - 0.594687 \times 0.518 = 0.8924493$$

There are a number of different models like the Z7 INE PAN model, where the analytical form is given by the following equation:

$$Z7\ INE\ PAN = 9.498X_1 + 3.566X_2 + 2.903X_3 + 0.452X_4 - 1.498$$

where:

X_1 – EBIT/total asset,

X_2 – equity/total assets,

X_3 – (profit after tax + depreciation)/total liabilities, and

X_4 – current assets/short term liabilities.

With the cut-off point placed at 0. A score above zero indicates a lack of default risk.

The models suffer from the assumption on the linear correlation, changes in the accounting standards, and cross-country differences with standards and practices. They should be applied as analytical tools for risk determination only.

The composite ratio detection model, due to its relative simplicity, is often used for the going concern assumption verification for financial statements auditing. Supervisory tools like capital requirements (BASEL, Solvency, EMIR[1]) are partly based on the ratio calculation.

Following are limitation of ratio analysis:

- GAAP dependency
- Lack of universal definition of ratios exempt from (capital requirements, P/E – price to earning)
- Changes of standards over time
- Lack of baseline between the companies (no standards even for very similar companies)
- Not suitable for professional decisions

---

[1] European Market Infrastructure Regulation (EMIR) is a European Union regulation designed to increase the stability of the over-the-counter (OTC) derivative markets throughout the EU states.

- Basic insight for the financial position
- Assumptions on the unqualified financial statements

Note: All analysis on the target entity should be done on the consolidated basis subject to meeting assumptions of well-known standards, unqualified opinion and up-to-date data.

5.13 SUMMARY

Information flows to the market from different sources. The data are different in respect of timing, frequency and reliability. Aggregate information on the financial market behavior is transmitted through the financial market indexes. The indexes are usually calculated as the average of the instruments in the basket. Data transmitted to the market impact the price of instruments. The valuation process takes into account different levels of data aggregation. The data are analyzed at the level of general economy, industry, and entity.

Financial statements constitute one of the significant sources of data for fundamental analysis. In order to enhance the reliability of the financial statements, they are subject to auditing procedures. The parent company reports both its own financial statements as well the consolidated financial statements, which shows all controlled assets.

Numerous ratios can be calculated on financial statements. Ratio analysis allows for comparison between entities. There are tools for failure predictions, which are based on the combination of ratios.

FURTHER READING

The basic Z score was presented in E. Altman (Altman, 1968). Practical issues regarding the comparability of financial statements is discussed in V. Cole et al. (Cole, Branson, & Breesch, 2011). The high frequency trading raises issues not only on technical but also on ethical matters, which is illustrated in M. Davis et al. paper (Davis, Kumiega, & Van Vliet, 2013).

Y/N QUESTIONS

Number	Question	Y/N
1	Financial statements are the most reliable data for the company.	Y/N

Number	Question	Y/N
2	The geometric average is used for calculation of all main indexes values.	Y/N
3	The data inflow on the stock exchange is used for valuation.	Y/N
4	Structure of competitor analysis is a part of industrial analysis.	Y/N
5	The managerial accounts are part of the financial statements.	Y/N
6	The IFRS is an auditing standard.	Y/N
7	The combination of the financial statement of the parent and subsidiary is called a consolidation.	Y/N
8	Current assets are equivalent to the sum of cash and depreciation.	Y/N
9	Z Score is sensitive to changes in accounting standards.	Y/N
10	A company controlled in the range of 20–49% is called a subsidiary.	Y/N

DISCUSSIONS

1. Using the mind map, revise the contents of the chapter.
2. On a sample of the financial statements of two companies from two different countries prepared based on different accounting standards, discuss the differences in financial statements, consider which differences are due to legal provision, best practice, market usage, and accounting policies.
3. Calculate a correlation between financial markets main indexes of two countries. Discuss the interconnectivity of markets.
4. Calculate a Z-score on a bankrupt company and a similar operating company; consider whether your cut-off value is appropriate.
5. Compare financial statements and stock exchange listings in terms of the reliability of data. Discuss the method for data quality enhancement.

SITUATION

Mark K.

Mark K. is an outstanding clerk involved in the protection of clients' rights. In his spare time, his hobby is accounting and finance. Mark has a good friend and this is you. Mark approaches you with the following issues:

Mark recently analyzed the reports of the CCC Ltd., after a friend of his had delivered the data as well as the audit opinion. Unfortunately, Mark did not understand what the audit opinion is for. Mark is deliberating the following issue: why is there an audit opinion for some financial statements and not for others? Mark has shown the opinion to you in its original language.

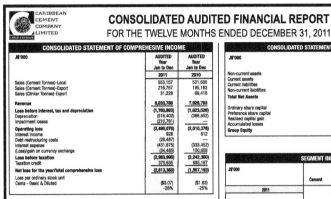

CONSOLIDATED AUDITED FINANCIAL REPORT
FOR THE TWELVE MONTHS ENDED DECEMBER 31, 2011

CARIBBEAN
CEMENT
COMPANY
LIMITED

A member of the TCL GROUP

REPORT OF THE INDEPENDENT AUDITORS ON THE SUMMARY CONSOLIDATED FINANCIAL STATEMENTS

To the Shareholders of Caribbean Cement Company Limited and its Subsidiaries

The accompanying summary consolidated financial statements, which comprise the summary consolidated statement of financial position as at 31 December 2011, and the summary consolidated statements of comprehensive income, changes in equity and cash flows for the year then ended, are derived from the audited consolidated financial statements of Caribbean Cement Company Limited and its Subsidiaries (the "Group") for the year ended 31 December 2011. We expressed a qualified audit opinion on those consolidated financial statements in our report dated 12 April 2012.

The summary consolidated financial statements do not contain all the disclosures required by International Financial Reporting Standards. Reading the summary consolidated financial statements, therefore is not a substitute for reading the audited consolidated financial statements of the Group.

Managements' Responsibility for the Summary Financial Statements
Management is responsible for the preparation of a summary of the audited consolidated financial statements, on the basis of their established criteria as described in Note 1 (see below).

Auditors' Responsibility
Our responsibility is to express an opinion on the summary consolidated financial statements based on our procedures, which were conducted in accordance with International Standard on Auditing (ISA) 810, "Engagements to Report on Summary Financial Statements."

Opinion
In our opinion, the summary consolidated financial statements derived from the audited consolidated financial statements of the Group for the year ended 31 December 2011 are consistent, in all material respects, with those consolidated financial statements. However, in our audit report dated 12 April 2012 in respect of the audited consolidated financial statements of the Group for the year ended 31 December 2011, our audit opinion was qualified for the matter described below.

In 2011 management recorded impairment losses pertaining to certain plant and machinery and deferred tax assets amounting to $193,292,000 and $618,391,000 respectively. These impairment losses were determined based on management's projections which assumed that the Group will generate significant revenue from exports to a certain market under a proposed agreement currently under active negotiation for which the terms and conditions have not been agreed as at the date of this audit report. We have not obtained sufficient appropriate

audit evidence to support the inclusion of the cashflows from these exports. Had management excluded these cashflows from its projections, the Group would have recognized an additional impairment loss of $784,886,000 in the statement of comprehensive income for the year then ended. The impact of this adjustment would reduce the carrying amount of plant and machinery, inventories (spares), deferred tax assets and shareholders' equity by $220,376,000, $67,874,000, $456,836,000 and $784,886,000, respectively. Additionally, the Group would have recorded a shareholders' deficiency amounting to $355,693,000 and net loss after tax of $3,378,246,000 as at 31 December 2011 and for the year then ended. Accordingly, the basic loss per ordinary stock unit would have been reported as ($3.97) for 2011. Our qualified audit opinion states that, except for the effects of the matter described, those financial statements give a true and fair view of the financial positions of the Group as at 31 December 2011, and of the Group's financial performance, changes in equity and cash flows for the year then ended in accordance with International Financial Reporting Standards and the requirements of the Jamaican Companies Act.

Emphasis of Matter
We draw attention to Note 5 in the summarized consolidated financial statements which indicates that the Group has reported accumulated losses of $4,152,955,000 as at 31 December 2011 and operating losses of $2,490,076,000 for the year then ended. In addition, the Group's net current liabilities amounted to $588,543,000 as at 31 December 2011. The accumulated losses, operating losses and net current liabilities have not been adjusted for the impact of the matters described in the Opinion paragraph above. These conditions, along with other matters as set forth in Note 5, indicate the existence of a material uncertainty which may cast significant doubt about the Group's ability to continue as a going concern. The financial statements have been prepared on the going concern basis because, as described in Note 5, the Group's management has embarked on a number of initiatives that, based on projections, demonstrate increases in revenue, cashflows and profitability of the Group, and hence improvement in the financial performance and position of the Group, for the year ending 31 December 2012 and beyond. In addition, Trinidad Cement Limited (the ultimate parent company), has also embarked on a debt restructuring exercise with the intention to provide the financing necessary to enable the Group to continue in business. Our opinion is not qualified in respect of this matter.

Chartered Accountants
Kingston, Jamaica
April 12, 2012

Source: *Caribbean Cement Company Limited, Investor relation, financial reports 2011.*
http://www.tclgroup.com/docs/default-document-library/cccl-financials---13-04-12.pdf

You are required to:

1. Explain the basic need for auditing.
2. Show to Mark who are the addresees of the opinion, the name of the audit company, which standard was selected to compose the financial statements and what standard was selected to perform the audit.
3. Assess the type of opinion issued – explain its meaning.
4. Explain to Mark the difference between the annual report and financial statements.
5. Assess if the level of materiality used by the auditor is higher or lower than 4 million dollars.
6. Calculate the return on sale ratio and discuss its reliability.

SOLUTION

1. The financial statements are prepared by the management of the company according to the publicly available rules. In a situation when the remuneration of the management is linked to the financial results (e.g., bonus on the year-end profit), then management has

incentives to adjust or apply rules which indicate a picture different from the reality. Such a situation constitutes a conflict of interests. Management cannot disclose all underlying data behind the financial statements (general ledger, documentation, registers, etc.) as it would jeopardize the competitive advantage of the company on the market. Therefore, there is a need for independent testing of the underlying data, by a person granted access to all the data but subject to confidentiality requirements and independence (auditor). The role of the auditor is to express opinion on the financial statements prepared by management, indicating whether or not those statements show a true and fair picture, in order to support users of the financial statements to take business decisions.

2. The addressees of the opinion are the shareholders of Caribbean Cement Company Limited and its subsidiaries. The opinion was expressed by Ernst and Young. The financial statements were presented in accordance with IFRS and the requirements of the Jamaica Companies Act. The auditor applied International Standards on Auditing.

3. The auditor qualified the financial statements and put an emphasis on matter without additional qualification.

4. The annual report is a document prepared by the management which summarizes the activity of the company, usually for a given year. This document may or may not include the full set of financial statements and auditors' opinon. A typical case is to include extracts from financial statements and auditor opinion on the financial statements. The data provided to you are not the financial statements or auditor opinon, but the annual report with extracts of the financial statements and information on auditor's opinion. Thus, not all data are shown, as they are in the financial statements.

5. Assess if the level of the materiality used by the auditor is higher or lower than 4 million dollars.

	J$'000	Range	Values	
Profit before tax	(2,983,995)	5–10%	Loss not applicable	
Total sales	8,033,786	1–1.5%	80,337	120,507
Total assets*	8,950,383	0.1–0.5%	8950	44,752
Equity	409,193	1–5%	4092	20,460
* Noncurrent assets 5,771,250 + Current assets 3,179,133.				

The smallest individually disclosed item on the opinion amounts to $87,674,000. Taking the above calculation and disclosure, the materiality applied by the auditor is likely to be higher than 4 million dollars. However, the actual calculation of materiality used by the auditor is subject to his professional judgment.

Based on financial statement:

$$ROS = \frac{EBIT}{Sales} = \frac{(2,490,076)}{8,033,786} = -31\%$$

After taking into account the opinion:

$$ROS = \frac{EBIT}{Sales} = \frac{(2,490,076 - 764,886)}{8,033,786} = \frac{(3,254,962)}{8,033,786} = -41\%$$

Net loss as per auditor (3,378,246), net loss as per financial statements (2,613,360), the difference is 764,886. The unadjusted calculation shows a better situation than the true picture by 9%.

Y/N QUESTIONS' ANSWERS

1	2	3	4	5	6	7	8	9	10
N	N	Y	Y	N	N	Y	N	Y	N

CHAPTER 6

Return and Risk Appraisal

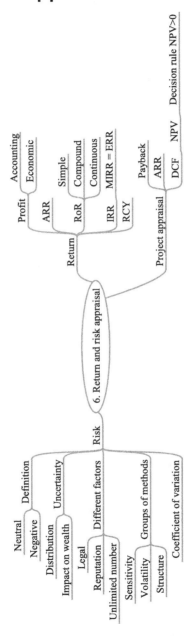

Finance: A Quantitative Introduction. http://dx.doi.org/10.1016/B978-0-12-801584-1.00006-8

6.1 RETURN

The basic goal of a firm is to make a financial return.

Financial return is another term for profit, but accountants and economists have different understandings of what constitutes profit. The return is usually presented as a percentage, whereas profit is given in money terms.

Accounting profit = revenues (sales) less identifiable costs.

Identifiable costs are those costs which can be identified, measured, and recorded (but do not include opportunity cost, etc.).

Economic profit = revenues (sales) less identifiable costs and opportunity costs (implicit costs).

Example:

The Blue Cafe bought a coffee machine for 10,000 euros which is used solely for making 1,000 cups of coffee, sold for 4 euros each. However, the machine is not making tea which could earn an expected net profit of 3,000 euros. What is the economic cost of the coffee machine?

Solution:

Cost of purchase	10,000
Implicit cost – foregone tea contribution	3,000
Total economic cost of the machine	13,000

When the economic concept of profit is used, we may prove that under perfect competition, a firm's goal for a long-term period is a profit of zero. This holds true because the profit is corrected with the risk premium.

Note that the economic implicit costs have the characteristic of potential revenues for accounting purposes.

Accounting profitability is subject to accounting standards (rules, e.g., US GAAP, UK GAAP, IFRS, PL GAAP; GAAP = Generally Accepted Accounting Procedures).

In addition to the economic and accounting profit, we differentiate tax profit which is used for calculating income tax. The profit for tax purposes is the accounting profit, adjusted for deductible and non-deductible items, according to the tax law – this is called a base for taxation. The accounting profit and base for taxation are usually substantially different, thus accounting uses the deferred tax adjustment to reconcile the timing differences between accounting and tax rules.

6.2 ACCOUNTING RATE OF RETURN

There is no single binding definition of accounting rate of return (ARR).

The widely used formulae are as follows:

$$\text{ARR} = \frac{\text{Estimated average profit}}{\text{Estimated average investment}} \times 100\% \qquad (6.1)$$

Instead of "average," definitions such as total or initial can be used.

$$\text{ARR} = \frac{\text{Estimated total profit}}{\text{Estimated initial investment}} \times 100\% \qquad (6.2)$$

$$\text{ARR} = \frac{\text{Estimated average profit}}{\text{Estimated initial investment}} \times 100\% \qquad (6.3)$$

Application of ARR: firstly we set the desired rate of return (RoR), then we calculate the projected RoR, if the projected ARR $>=$ desired ARR, then we accept the project.

Example:

A venture capital company considers investing in a small ice-cream company. The company undertakes projects with an ARR above 14%. The initial investment is 100k euros, the depreciation period is 5 years (linear) and the expected profits before depreciation charge are 25, 20, 30, 40, 20k euros for the next 5 years respectively.

Should the venture capitalist proceed with financing the project?

Solution:

Year	Profit after capital charge	Mid-year BV*	ARR for the year
	Euros, profit less depreciation charge (k euros)	Euros (000)	%
1	5	90	5.5
2	0	70	0
3	10	50	10
4	20	30	66.6
5	0	10	0
BV = book value.			

Only in year 4 does the project ARR exceed the target ARR, therefore there is no basis for a yes or no answer as to whether or not to make the investment.

Thus, the investor should calculate the ARR for the whole 5-year period.

Total profit for the period		135
Depreciation charge		(100)
Net profit		35
Annual average profit		7
Initial investments		100
Average net book value over 5-year period	100 + 0/5 = 20	20
ARR = Average annual profit to average net book value	7/20	35%
Values inside parentheses indicate negative.		

Based on the above calculation, the project should be accepted.

Consider:

What is the obvious drawback of ARR?

Solution:

Time value of money.

The RoR is expressed in percentage thus, it is similar to the interest rate used for the time value of money (see Appendix A). The RoR is used both for assessment of the project viability and comparison of projects. Because the RoR can be calculated for different time intervals it behaves similarly to the interest rate as used for the time value of money calculation. Let us explain the formula for RoR in an example.

Example:

John invested 200 euros into a project and received 220 euros after 2 years. What is the RoR of the project?

Solution:

$$\text{RoR} = \frac{\text{future value}}{\text{present value}} = \frac{220}{200} = 1.1$$

This formula does not represent a percentage because it considers the initial value of the investment, thus to come to a percentage value we need to deduct "1." The RoR is = 1.1 − 1 = 10%.

The calculated RoR is still time dependent as it shows the return for 2 years. Usually we use the annual rate for discounting and time value calculations. As a result the true formula is as follows:

$$\text{RoR} = \frac{1}{n}\left(\frac{\text{future value}}{\text{present value}} - 1\right),$$ where n is the number of years and by simplifying the notation we arrive at:

$$\text{RoR} = \frac{1}{n}\left(\frac{\text{FV}}{\text{PV}} - 1\right),$$ therefore John earned an annual RoR of 5%.

The hidden assumption in the above example was that John is using a simple capitalization rule. However, John can use the compound or continuous capitalization rule. Therefore, the method of calculation of the RoR would be different depending on the underlying capitalization rule used. The formulae are thus as follows:

Type of capitalization	Simple capitalization	Compound capitalization	Continuous capitalization
Formula of RoR	$\frac{1}{n}\left(\frac{\text{FV}}{\text{PV}} - 1\right)$	$\left(\frac{\text{FV}}{\text{PV}}\right)^{\frac{1}{n}} - 1$	$\frac{1}{n}(\ln\text{FV} - \ln\text{PV})$
Name	Simple RoR	Effective RoR	Logarithmic RoR
Notation	RoR	RoR_e	RoR_l

Note that these formulae are similar to different types of calculation of averages (simple or geometric).

Let us continue John's case. What would be the effective and logarithmic rates of return?

Effective =	Logarithmic =
$\left(\frac{220}{200}\right)^{\frac{1}{2}} - 1$ which is = 4.8%	$\frac{1}{n}(\ln 220 - \ln 200) = 4.7\%$

Note that the logarithmic RoR is the smallest one.

To sum up, we may say that John will earn 5%, 4.8%, or 4.7% annually based on the underlying capitalization assumption.

Another hidden assumption used in *Public registers* and *Data feeds* was that the initial investment earns a gain after the investment period. But it may be the case that the invested capital yields additional cash flows.

Example:

You bought a share for 100 euros, but after 1 year you got 10 euros dividend, and after 2 years you sell your share for 130 euros;

Thus a simple calculation such as $\dfrac{\left((10+130)/100\right)-1}{2}$ is misleading because it assumes that the earned 10 euros of dividend was not invested at all (a simple capitalization rule), but in fact your dividend can be placed into bank deposit for a given interest rate i.

The interest rate "i" above could be defined annually, semi-annually, and so on, and could be stable in time or change over time, for example, stochastically. For practical reasons, it is assumed that the capitalization period reflects the frequency of the cash flows (in our case, dividends are paid annually, thus the annual capitalization period is used), and additional cash flows are reinvested with the same RoR as achieved on the project. Bearing in mind the above assumption, the calculation reduces itself to finding the IRR (technicalities are compared in Appendix A).

The IRR is defined as follows:

$$\text{IRR} = \sum_{t=1}^{n} \frac{C_t}{(1+\text{IRR})^t} = I_0 \quad \text{Which is equivalent to:} \qquad (6.4)$$

$$\sum_{t=1}^{n} C_t (1+\text{IRR})^{n-t} = I_0 (1+\text{IRR})^n$$

where

C_t = cash flow for time t and

I_0 = initial investment.

Consequently the right-hand equation shows the relation of the future value of cash flows from the project to the initial investment. The sum of the cash flows in given periods is its future value at the IRR rate, thus:

$\text{FV} = \sum_{t=1}^{n} C_t (1+\text{IRR})^{n-t}$, and PV = I_0 then by rearrangement of the right-hand equation, we arrive at:

$$\text{FV} = \text{PV}(1+\text{IRR})^n \qquad (6.5)$$

This means that:

$$\text{IRR} = \left(\frac{\text{FV}}{\text{PV}}\right)^{\frac{1}{n}} - 1 \qquad (6.6)$$

which is the effective RoR under the assumption that cash flows are re-invested at the IRR rate.

Example:

You bought a share for 100 euros, but after 1 year you get 10 euros as a dividend, and after the second year you get 20 euros as a dividend. The following year, you sell your share for 130 euros. What is the RoR?

Solution:

First of all the IRR for current cash flows must be stated:

$$RoR_e = IRR = \sum_{t=1}^{n} \frac{C_t}{(1+IRR)^t} = I_0$$

Thus,

$$\frac{10}{(1+IRR)^1} + \frac{20}{(1+IRR)^1} + \frac{130}{(1+IRR)^1} = 100$$

By sorting this equation (the approximation or trial error procedure – more details in Appendix A), we arrive at

IRR = 18.85% which is a desirable RoR.

There is no need to limit the reinvestment rate to the IRR of the project. The equation:

$$\sum_{t=1}^{n} C_t(1+IRR)^{n-t} = I_0(1+IRR)^n \tag{6.7}$$

can be rewritten to a more general form

$$\sum_{t=1}^{n} C_t(1+i_r)^{n-t} = I_0(1+IRR)^n \tag{6.8}$$

where i_r represents the rate at which the cash flow was reinvested, thus by a rearrangement of the formula, we arrive at the external rate of return (ERR) or modified internal rate of return (MIRR), this is:

$$MIRR = ERR = \left(\frac{\sum_{t=1}^{n} C_t(1+i_r)^{n-t}}{I_0} \right)^{\frac{1}{n}} - 1 \tag{6.9}$$

The modified **IRR** assumes that positive cash flows are reinvested at the firm's cost of capital, and the initial outlays are financed at the firm's financing cost. Therefore, **MIRR** reflects more accurately the cost and profitability of a given project.

The simplified formula for **MIRR** is:

$$\sqrt[n]{\frac{FV\left(positive\ cashflow\ at\ cost\ of\ capital\right)}{PV\left(Initial\ outflow,\ financing\ costs\right)}} - 1 \qquad (6.10)$$

Example:

Take a 2-year project with an initial outlay of 195,000 euros and a cost of capital of 12% that will give a return of 121,000 euros in the first year and 131,000 euros in the second year. We need to find the **IRR** of the project so that the net present value (NPV) = 0:

NPV = 0 = − 195,000 + 121,000/(1+ **IRR**) + 131,000/(1 + **IRR**)²

NPV = 0 when **IRR** = 18.66%

To calculate the **MIRR** of the project, we have to assume that the positive cash flows will be reinvested at a 12% cost of capital. So the future value of the positive cash flows is computed as:

121,000(1.12) + 131,000 = 266,520 = Future value of positive cash flows at $t = 2$

Now divide the future value of the cash flows by the present value of the initial outlay (compare 6.10 above), which was 195,000 euros, and find the geometric return for 2 periods.

$$\sqrt{266,520/195,000} - 1 = 16.91\%\ MIRR$$

The 16.91% **MIRR** is lower than the **IRR** of 18.66%.

Both **IRR** and **MIRR** assume that the interest rate is fixed, but more generally it can be considered as a situation where the cash flows are reinvested at different rates. In such a case, the future value of the investment is given by the following formula:

$$FV\sum_{t=1}^{n}C_t(1+i_{t+1})(1+i_{t+2})(1+i_{t+3})...(1+i_n) \qquad (6.11)$$

Consequently the present value of such a cash flow is given by:

$$PV = \sum_{t=1}^{n} \frac{C_t}{(1+i_1)\ldots(1+i_t)} \tag{6.12}$$

Thus, the MIRR formula changes to the so-called realized compound yield (RCY), where the reinvestment rate is changing over time.

$$RCY = \left(\frac{\sum_{t=1}^{n} C_t (1+i_1)\ldots(1+i_t)}{I_0} \right)^{\frac{1}{n}} - 1 \tag{6.13}$$

If the future cash inflows are infinite, the RoR is the rate of payments against the present value of the perpetuity. The formula is given by:

$$RoR = \frac{PMT}{PV} \tag{6.14}$$

In case of steady increase of the annuity installment by the rate of growth (g), the formula is modified as follows:

$$RoR = \frac{PMT(1+g)}{PV} + g \tag{6.15}$$

where PMT is the present value of annuity installments and PV is the present value of the perpetuity.

Example:

A disability pension of 300 euros yearly is offered with a price of 6,000 euros.

1. What is the RoR on that product?

2. How does the return change if the installment is increased by 7% each year?

Solution:

1. $RoR = \dfrac{300}{6,000} = 5\%$

2. $RoR = \dfrac{300(1+7\%)}{6,000} + 0.07 = 12.35\%$

The above reasoning is also used for establishing the prices of the assets on the market:

$$\text{Suppose the return} = \frac{\text{present value of future payments}}{\text{investment value}}$$

so in the case of investment into shares with an undefined investment period and assumed stable future dividends, the RoR (r) is equal to:

$$r = \frac{\text{future dividends}}{\text{share price}} = \frac{D_1}{P_0} \qquad (6.16)$$

With an expected steady growth in dividends it is:

$$r = \frac{\text{future dividends}}{\text{share price}} = \frac{D_1}{P_0} + g \qquad (6.17)$$

Then the price of the shares (by rearrangement of the above) is:

$$P_0 = \frac{D_1}{r} \qquad (6.18)$$

or if with growth (g)

$$P_0 = \frac{D_1}{r - g} \qquad (6.19)$$

The steady increase in dividends allows us to state that $D_1 = D_0(1 + g)$ thus

$$P_0 = \frac{D_0(1 + g)}{r - g} \qquad (6.20)$$

The above equation demonstrates the relationship between the price and RoR of a share (a residual instrument).

6.3 SIMPLE PROJECT ASSESSMENT

6.3.1 The Payback Method
Payback is the method used to assess how long it would take a project to pay back the initial investment.

		Accumulated profit
Initial investment	100,000	
Profit before depreciation		
Year 1	(10,000)	(10,000)
Year 2	30,000	20,000
Year 3	80,000	100,000
Year 4	20,000	120,000
Values inside parentheses indicate negative.		

At the end of year 3, the initial investment is repaid.

A typical mistake when calculating the payback period and ARR is to take the profit after depreciation – why?

These methods do not take into account the time value of money.

6.3.2 Discounted Cash Flow (DCF) Method

Contrary to the ARR and payback method the DCF does take into account the time value of money.

Example:

Imagine you have 100 euros that you put into a savings account for 2 years at 5% fixed interest rate. What would you earn after two years? And how much would you have to put into the bank account to with-draw 100 euros after 2 years?

Solution:

1. In the first year you earn 100 + 5% of 100, giving a total of 105. You might choose to either withdraw the interest after the first year or decide to attach it to the capital and reinvest the total at the agreed rate of 5% (note that the percentage is always given as p.a. = per annum – annual rate).
   Say that you decided to reinvest interest and capital, in the second year you would earn:

   $$105 + 105 \times 5\% = 105 + 5.25 = 110.25$$

   This means that after two years of investment, with compound interest, you get 110.25 euros.
   In case you had withdrawn the interest earned after the first year instead of reinvesting and had cashed the 5 euros – what would be your gain in the second year – would it be 5 euros too?

2. To earn 100 euros in total after two years, we have to solve an equation:

   $$X + X \text{ times } 5\% + (X + X \text{ times } 5\%) \text{ times } 5\% = 100$$

This stands for capital	Those are the interest in year 1	The capital year 2 times interest	Capital thereafter
X	X times 5%	$(X + X$ times 5%) times 5%	= 100

Thus, the solution is:

$$X + 5\%X + 5\%X + 5\%^2 X = 100$$
$$X(1 + 5\%) + X(5\% + 5\%^2) = 100$$
$$X(1 + 5\% + 5\% + 5\%^2) = 100$$
$$X = 100/1.1025$$
$$X = 90.70$$

Check:

First year interest on 90.7 capital is: $90.70 \times 0.05 = 4.53$

Second year interest after reinvestment of capital and first year interest $(90.70 + 4.53) \times 0.05 = 4.76$

Total value $(90.70 + 4.53 + 4.76) = 99.99$

Difference $(100 - 99.99 - \text{round up differences})$

For details on the time value of money, refer to Appendix A.

6.3.3 NPV Method

The NPV method takes into account the time value of money.

Example:

		Discount factor @ 12%	Present value
Initial investment	(100,000)	1	(100,000)
Profit before depreciation			
Year 1	(10,000)	0.893	(8,930)
Year 2	30,000	0.797	23,910
Year 3	80,000	0.712	56,960
Year 4	20,000	0.636	12,720
NPV of project			(15,340)
Values inside parentheses indicate negative.			

The decision criteria for NPV:

1. Positive – accept
2. Negative – reject
3. Zero – irrelevant

In this case, the NPV is negative; therefore, this project should be rejected.

Consider: What would be the discount rate to make the NPV equal to zero?

The cash flow projection should be consistent either in nominal or real values.

For nominal cash flow, a nominal rate is used but for real cash flow the real rate is used. It is a typical error in an NPV calculation to apply the nominal rate to real cash flow or vice versa.

A year 0 term: it is used to denote the initial outflow (seldom inflows) at the moment of starting the project, for example, fixed asset expenditure.

The cash flow assessment is sensitive for a number of reasons:

1. Opportunity costs
2. Investor's individual preferences
3. Inflation
4. Risks and distribution of conditional cash flows

The effect of inflation is significant and affects both cash flow and the cost of capital.

Not all components of cash flow will necessarily increase at the same inflation rate, for example, gas, oil, and real estate.

Inflation itself is affected by the inflation expectation of the market.

6.4 RISK

Risk has no formal definition.

There are two following approaches to characterize risk:

1. Neutral = not meeting the target
2. Negative = chance of loss

6.4.1 Risk and Uncertainty

Risk = possible to measure (known distribution)

Uncertainty = impossible to measure (unknown distribution)

There is another distinction between risk and uncertainty. A risk situation for an individual is when the uncertainty relating to the situation may affect his or her individual wealth.

Consider:

Mark is a sole trader in construction and is about to enter into a contract to construct a house for 600,000 euros, payable in 2 months' time. He can build houses if the temperature outdoors is above 5°C. He is unsure about the weather. If it is colder than 5°C, Mark will not be able to work and he will make a loss, otherwise he will be able to gain from the contract.

John is a teacher and he is also unsure about the weather. If it is below 5°C, he will conduct lectures in the lecture room, otherwise he will conduct his lectures outside.

How does the situation differ for Mark and John?

Solution:

Mark faces a risk situation, whereby the realization of the scenario (i.e., it is colder than 5°C) affects his wealth, whereas John faces uncertainty, as the realization of the scenario does not affect his wealth.

Risk in legislation – being responsible on the basis of risk versus responsibility on the basis of damage caused. There is a different understanding of risk in finance compared with legal science.

Risk is also meant as the mental ability to act on predictions of future events.

Risk in terms of financial analysis ends up with the cash outflow. Thus, there is no financial risk if we cannot convert the source of risk into the cash flows.

Risk is usually defined by a risk factor, for example, currency risk, market risk, default risk, and so on. The other approach to risk is to assess the changeability of the output. Thus, there are three basic concepts of risk assessment:

- volatility – analysis of the risky output,
- sensitivity – analysis of factors having an impact on the risk,
- structure mismatch – reduces structure into risk value.

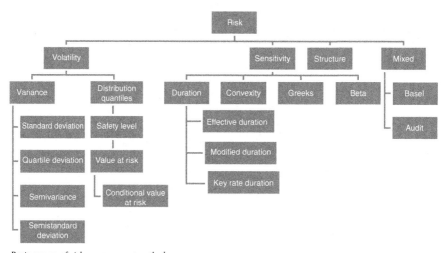

Basic groups of risk measurement methods

The different risk measurement methods are usually used for different instruments, duration is typically used for bonds, Greeks for options, whereas beta is a risk measure for a portfolio. The description of the specific methods are linked to the groups of theories or instruments; they are discussed in their relevant sections.

Example:

List different examples of risk measurement, together with the arguments for and against each one.

Solution:

Type of Measure	Description	Advantages	Disadvantages
Standard deviation (variance square root)	Shows average distance to mean	Easy to use, well-known form of statistical measurement	Captures a neutral concept of risk
Derivative	Shows the impact of small changes to input against output	Well-known in mathematics (a limit)	It shows only changes and behavior for small changes, it is not feasible for long-term analysis
Value at risk	Shows risk as the value which is unlikely to be exceeded	Can capture different instruments together, easy to explain	Difficult to measure on a continuous basis if simulation must be applied
Mismatch of structure	Tries to capture divergences from a given pattern	Applicable for complex issues	Measurement is subject to a judgmental decision

Coefficient of variation is a combined method of measuring both return and risk. It follows the following formula:

$$CV = \frac{\sigma}{\text{Expected return}} \tag{6.21}$$

where σ denotes the standard deviation of returns, and expected return is assumed not to be negative.

An object (instrument, project) can be characterized by a vector (return, variance of return), where return is the measurement of profitability and variance is the measurement of risk. Thus, the most profitable projects are those with the highest return and the lowest variance.

Example:

A share in ABC plc has the following returns: 5, 10, 11, 5, –6. A share in WRS plc has the following returns: 7, 2, 15, 4, 17. Which share is more risky?

Solution:

An average return of the shares:

ABC plc = (5 + 10 + 11 + 5 − 6)/5 = 5

WRS plc = (7 + 2 + 15 + 4 + 17)/5 = 45/5 = 9

The variance of the returns is:

ABC plc = $(5 − 5)^2 + (10 − 5)^2 + (11 − 5)^2 + (5 − 5)^2 + (−6 − 5)^2$ /5
   = 0 + 25 + 36 + 0 + 121/5 = 182/5 = 36.4

WRS plc = $(7 − 9)^2 + (2 − 9)^2 + (15 − 9)^2 + (4 − 9)^2 + (17 − 9)^2$ /5
   = 4 + 49 + 36 + 25 + 64 = 178/5 = 35.6

Thus:

(ABC plc) 36.4 > 35.6 (WRS plc)

The ABC plc share is the more risky.

Note that the method of variance approach does not define the period under review; it is a judgmental (arbitrary) decision.

6.5 SUMMARY

Profit orientation is a generally accepted assumption for financial analysis of companies. Return is expressed as a fraction, whereas profit is a value expressed in money terms. Accounting and economic profits are different. The concept of accounting profit varies between different systems of GAAP. ARR is not strictly defined. ARR and payback period do not take into account the time value of money. There are different methods of RoR calculation depending on the type of capitalization of return. DCF method (NPV) is popular for valuation of instruments and projects due to the fact that it takes into account the time value of money. An alternative for assessing the viability of the project in addition to the NPV calculation is IRR. IRR and NPV do not necessarily provide the same conclusion for any given cash flow. Risk has no formal definition; risk is a situation-driven concept. Uncertainty and risk are different, both in terms of their quantification and their impact on one's wealth. There are different methods of risk assessment. The basic group of methods relates to volatility, sensitivity and structure.

Coefficient of variation is an example of a combination of both risk and return.

FURTHER READING

A discussion on risk and uncertainty is provided by F. Knight (1921). The link between uncertainty, risk and quality is demonstrated by G. Akerlof (1970). A short review of basic trend development can be found in M. Miller (1999). An overview of the development of risk attitude in accounting and finance is presented by M. Power (2004). The major risk factors for bonds and stocks are analyzed by E. Fama and K. French (1993).

Y/N QUESTIONS

Number	Question	Y/N
1	ARR is equal to RoE	Y/N
2	The IRR assumes that the cash flows are reinvested at the cost of capital.	Y/N
3	IRR and MIRR assume fixed interest rates.	Y/N
4	NPV is equal to PV if IRR is equal to zero.	Y/N
5	Derivative is a tool for a long-term risk effect measurement.	Y/N
6	Value at risk simulation is a time consuming activity.	Y/N
7	The interest rate is 5%, the inflation rate is 3%, the real rate is thus 8%.	Y/N
8	Greeks are used for the risk assessment of options.	Y/N
9	Opportunity costs are measured as replacement costs.	Y/N
10	The return is expressed in money.	Y/N

DISCUSSIONS

1. Using the mind map, review the contents of the chapter.
2. Prove the relation that $RoR_l = \ln(1 + RoR_e)$.
3. Discuss the risk measurement methods: VAR, variance, standard deviation, sensitivity in the context of two groups of risk definition; neutral and negative.
4. Discuss the common sense understanding of risk in your home and host countries – do you see any differences?
5. The disability pension of €200 yearly is offered with the price of €3,000. What is the return if in each year the installment will be increased by 2%?

SITUATION

Zakopane

Two mountaineers, Jankiel and Janosik, operate the sole business sales points in Zakopane on the famous Krupówki Street.

Jankiel loves high mountain-walking and sells sunglasses to tourists. Based on his experience, sales are strongly connected to the weather, which can be sunny or rainy. If it is sunny then he earns 300 PLN in a day, if it rains he makes only 50 PLN in a day. During the course of a year, approximately 60% of days are rainy and 40% of days are sunny.

Some years ago, Janosik was a professional swimmer and he believes that tourists should not get wet, because in Zakopane it is easy to get cold. Janosik sells raincoats. If it rains, Janosik earns 200 PLN in daily profits and if it is sunny he earns 75 PLN in daily profits.

Both Janosik and Jankiel have to pay taxes in a lump sum every month and become frustrated that once they have paid their tax contribution, they are sometimes forced to make use of expensive overdraft facilities from GoodBank in order to maintain a healthy cash flow.

You are required to:

1. State the expected profits separately for both sole traders, including their risk profile.
2. Advise on what can they do to satisfy the Tax Office.

SOLUTION

1.

State	Sun	Rain	Average Income	Cash Flow Risk
Probability	0.4	0.6		
Sunglasses	300	50	120 + 30 = 150	High
Raincoats	75	200	30 + 120 = 150	High

The cash flow risk is high because both suffer from days with high and low daily cash inflow.

2. If they share their businesses according to ratio of sunny to rainy days (i.e., 40–60) and if Jankiel sells raincoats in addition to sunglasses

and Janosik sells sunglasses alongside raincoats, then when it is sunny they will each get 150 PLN (300 × 0.4 + 75 × 0.4) and rainy 150 PLN (50 × 0.6 + 200 × 0.6).

Now

State	Sun	Rain	Average Income	Cash Flow Risk
Probability	0.4	0.6		
Both	150	150	150	Low

Now both Jankiel and Janosik earn in average as much as before, but the risk to their cash flow is low. The Tax Office is satisfied whilst Good-Bank becomes sad.

Y/N QUESTIONS' ANSWERS

1	2	3	4	5	6	7	8	9	10
N	Y	Y	N	N	Y	N	Y	N	N

CHAPTER 7

Money Market and Liquidity Management

Finance: A Quantitative Introduction. http://dx.doi.org/10.1016/B978-0-12-801584-1.00007-X

7.1 MONEY MARKET

Money market – the market for liquid assets.

The primary goal of the money market is to provide working capital to the entities. The money market does not have a standard structure and one place of operation; typically it is an OTC market.

Capital employed definition: total assets less total liabilities and provision for liabilities.

Working capital definition: current assets less current liabilities.

Note: Working capital is á term with its origin in accounting, thus it is subject to accounting standards. In accounting, "current" usually means repayable in less than a year. Taking this definition, a long-term loan has a short-term part too.

7.2 WORKING CAPITAL CYCLE

Working capital flows though different stages.

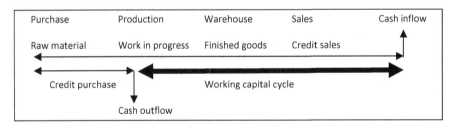

The average working capital cycle period is calculated as the sum of the collection period, inventory days, and average creditor period. Therefore, we may define it as follows:

Collection period		$\dfrac{\text{Debtors}}{\text{Sales (credit)}} \times 365$	Days
Inventory days	Finished goods	$\dfrac{\text{Finished goods}}{\text{Cost of sales}} \times 365$	Days
	W.I.P.	$\dfrac{\text{Work in progress}}{\text{Cost of production}} \times 365$	Days
	Raw materials	$\dfrac{\text{Raw materials}}{\text{Raw material purchase}} \times 365$	Days

Average creditor period		$\dfrac{\text{Payables}}{\text{Purchase (credit)}} \times 365$	Days
	Working capital cycle in days		$\sum$ Days

For a physical person, working capital constitutes the surplus or deficit between cash inflows and outflows for a given period.

The need for substantial liquidity arises when an entity increases sales without appropriate investment to its asset base. Such a squeeze on assets may result in overtrading.

The major activity on the money market is the provision of short-term loans and short-term money deposits.

The demand for money market instruments is strongly linked to the excess cash available on the market. For major financial institutions, this is linked to the policy of the central bank, mainly the compulsory reserve rate.

The statement "short-term" can be as short as overnight; this implies that in order to realize a significant benefit from such a transaction, the amounts which have to be invested are considerable (e.g., several millions, billions, etc.). Because of transaction costs and the size of the transaction, the money market is stimulated mainly by the financial institutions and blue chips (corporations with a national reputation for quality, reliability, and the ability to operate profitably in good and bad times). There is, nevertheless, a fraction of money market opportunities for retail clients, mainly through credit cards and electronic short-term deposits.

7.3 CLASSIFICATION

Money market classification:

Criteria	Type	Notes
Size of the transaction	Wholesale market (central market) or interbank	Typically over-the-counter between financial institutions
	Retail market	Mainly banks granting loans to customers

Criteria	Type	Notes
Territory	Local level Country level International level	
Participant	Inter bank Companies Individuals	

7.4 INSTRUMENTS

Typical instruments of the money market are following:

- Short-term deposits and short-term loans: overnight, 1 week, 2 weeks, 1 month, 3 months, 6 months, 1 year
- T-bill, short-term bonds issued by the government with different maturities
- Commercial papers – short-term bonds issued by well-recognized, usually internationally reputable companies
- Bills of exchange
- Commercial liabilities – transactions based on the general principles of the civil law, which are not securities
- Securities backed-up with the existing or expected receivables (securitization)
- Deposit certificates – securities drawn based on a negotiable deposit, in contrast to a classical deposit, which is linked to a specific person
- Credit cards

The difference between commercial papers and bills of exchange lies primarily in their legal framework. Commercial papers are usually issued in accordance with bond law. In consequence, the issuer has an information obligation, such as a memorandum (a short version of a prospectus), whereas bills of exchange are issued in accordance with bill law, which does not require additional disclosure.

Consider:

Which instrument is more risky to the investor: bill of exchange or bond?

Back up your view with an example.

Hint:

Consider the effect of additional information provided via the bonds issue, which is offset by the relatively quick collection of the debt in the case of bills of exchange.

There are following three major factors influencing the price of a financial instrument:

1. Central bank reference rates
2. Supply and demand
3. The risk of default (called the "credit risk")

The instruments issued by governments or central banks are viewed as being close to zero risk of default, whereas those issued by small, weak companies are perceived as speculative and risky. The nature of the money market is rather to deal with the short-term and not risky instruments (like deposits). Estimation of credit risk is usually done with reference to ratings issued by rating agencies like Standard & Poor's.

7.5 RATES

The central bank rate is a rate at which the central bank is prepared to lend short-term money to the bank. This is a nominal rate, meaning that it includes inflation. This rate is usually at the same time a ceiling for the money market rate. A commercial bank may offer its excess money to another bank which actually needs liquidity; however, to be more competitive than the central bank, the commercial bank should offer a lower rate than the central bank. This is a general rule but in some situations it may not hold true due to different distortions (e.g., central bank policy, changes in rating).

The difference between an interbank loan and central bank loan is that with an interbank loan the total amount of money available to the economy remains unchanged while a loan from central bank increases the money supply. This increase in money supply may translate into an inflation pressure.

Because the offers and bids placed between the banks are performed on an over-the-counter basis, the rest of the market is not informed unless a benchmark is set. The interbank dealers of the major banks provide their bids and ask for offers to an information provider (e.g., Reuters). Separate averages for all bids and all ask offers are calculated. The interbank offered rates and bid rates are announced at an agreed moment in time. The most common indexes are the following:

- LIBOR – London Interbank Offer Rate
- LIBID – London Interbank Bid Rate

There are other similar indexes in major countries, they are used to quote different instruments.

The price of a loan or deposit is expressed as the rate (rate of interest). The market custom is to quote a rate per annum.

The interest rate can be either fixed or floating.

The interbank market distinguishes between short- and long-term deposits. Short-term deposits are those payable up to one month, long-term are from month to 1 year.

Types of one day deposit:

1. Overnight (O/N) – starts on the day of the transaction and ends the next day.
2. Tomnext (T/N) [tomorrow next] – starts the day after the day of the transaction and ends the next day.
3. Spot next (S/N) – starts the first working day after the day of the transaction and ends the next day.

Non-1-day deposits are usually classed as spot next.

Government securities: these are used for short-term liquidity financing or for a long-term budget deficit financing. There are different names in different countries for this kind of instrument. The typical terms are: T-bills (Treasury bills), government bonds or treasury bonds, treasury notes, etc. They are usually divided in two groups based on their maturity: T-bills are money market instruments and mature in up to 12 months. Treasury bonds and treasury notes are recognized as long-term investments traded on the capital market.

Treasury notes are issued with maturities of one, three, five, seven, and 10 years, whereas treasury bonds (also called "long bonds") offer maturities of 20 and 30 years. In this case, the only difference between notes and bonds is their length of maturity. The 10-year Treasury note is the most widely used; it is used as both the benchmark for the treasury market and as the basis for banks' calculation of mortgage rates.

7.6 PRICING

Another difference between the treasury instruments is their pricing. T-bills are sold at a discount to par (face, nominal value). Treasury notes and bonds pay a traditional "coupon," or interest payment (e.g., every 6 months).

Example:

The government is willing to finance a short-term credit requirement and offers a 100 million T-bill at the discount of 5%. This means that the market players will buy the 100 million par value at the price of 95 million and after the maturity (e.g., 4 months) the government will repay 100 million.

In contrast, the government may offer 100 million notes due in two years sold with 5% p.a. meaning that in the first year, the government will pay 5 million, and in the second year it will pay 5 million interest and capital of 100 million (assuming no capitalization).

A discount on T-bill is the difference between the par value and value offered.

$$D = P - M \tag{7.1}$$

where

D = discount,

P = par value, and

M = market value.

The amount of discount can be expressed as an annual rate:

$$d = (D / P) \times (360 / n) \times 100\% \tag{7.2}$$

where

d = discount rate per annum, and

n = number of days between the day of purchase and the repayment day at maturity.

Note that 360 represents 360 days and it is a convention for a year. In practice, the calculation can use 365 days, or another figure as its basis, thus discounting rates are sensitive to their calculation base.

By replacing par value (P) with market value (M), the annual return on the T-bill is given as:

$$r = (D/M) \times (360/n) \times 100\%$$

r = annualized return rate of the T-bill.

The r shows the income rate of the specific bill for the entire year; it is used to compare different instruments with different maturities.

By rearranging the above equation, the value of discount amounts to:

$$D = P \times (d/100) \times (n/360) \tag{7.3}$$

assuming d is given.

By the combination of $r = (D/M) \times (360/n) \times 100\%$ and $D = P - M$, we obtain:

$$M = P \Big/ \left[\frac{rn}{360 \times 100} + 1 \right] \tag{7.4}$$

formula for the market price of a T-bill, where r is given.

Example:

The government wants to place the issue of 100 million euros, due within 3 months, into the market. The offer is announced to a number of banks. The price which allows making the entire placement is 97 million.

You are required to:

1. Calculate the value of the discount
2. Calculate the discount rate

3. Calculate the return for seller and buyer having sold/bought the entire issue after 30 days for 99 million
4. Calculate the purchase and selling price of a T-bill of nominal value of 100,000 euros with 60 days of maturity when the bid return is 10.23% per annum, and the ask return price is 11.43%

Solution:

1. $D = 100 - 97 = 3$ million discount
2. $d = (D/P) \times (360/n) \times 100\% = 3/100 \times 360/90 \times 100\% = 12\%$

Buyer returns position:

$r = (D/M) \times (360/n) \times 100\% = (100 - 99)/99 \times 360/60 \times 100\% = 6\%$

Seller returns position:

$r = (D/M) \times (360/n) \times 100\% = (99 - 97)/97 \times 360/30 \times 100\% = 25\%$

Purchase price:

$$M = P \bigg/ \left[\frac{rn}{360 \times 100} + 1\right] = 100,000/(1 + 60 \times 0.1143/360)$$
$$= 98,130.61 - \text{ask market price.}$$

Selling price:

$$M = P \bigg/ \left[\frac{rn}{360 \times 100} + 1\right] = 100,000/(1 + 60 \times 0.1023/360)$$
$$= 98,323.58 - \text{bid market price.}$$

Other similar activities for liquidity management are the following:

- Factoring – providing liquidity secured with current assets (usually stock, work in progress, or finished goods)
- Forfeiting – providing liquidity secured with international bills of exchange.

7.7 CURRENT ISSUES

Because of changes to the business on financial markets caused by the introduction of MiFID (Markets in Financial Instruments Directive) and transparency requirements, the competition factor on the financial markets become noninterest rate charges as the source of income for the companies and banks. Competitive advantage is built up by the introduction of different types of charges and surcharges to the transaction. As a response to this trend, some legislation systems lay down the obligation to inform the customer about the effective interest rate, which actually takes into account all charges and costs.

7.8 SUMMARY

The money market is used to finance liquidity. Liquidity is the ability to satisfy the liabilities at due time. The basic measurement of liquidity is working capital. Working capital is the difference between current assets and current liabilities, it shows current financial needs. In contrast, capital employed is the difference between total assets and total liabilities and provision for liabilities – it is a long-term financing of activities.

The working capital cycle is the conversion of outflow payments into inflow payments. Typically, the working capital cycle is calculated in days as the sum of days for subsequent cash conversion, beginning with creditor's days and ending with debtor's days.

The money market does not have a standard structure and one place of operation; typically it is an OTC market. Typical instruments on the money market include short-term loans, T-bills and commercial papers. To monitor the market, an average rate is benchmarked by the main players, a typical reference index is, for example, LIBOR. A significant player on the money market is the government and the central bank. As a matter of custom, the valuation of instruments on the money market is based on the simple interest rate. Besides the direct financing of liquidity from the money market, there are other tools available for companies, for example, factoring or forfeiting.

FURTHER READING

A discussion on the microstructure of the European money market can be found in P. Hartmann et al. (Hartmann, Manna, & Manzanares, 2001). Analysis of the factors influencing the increase of spreads on money markets is shown by J. Taylor and J. Williams (2009).

Y/N QUESTIONS

Number	Question	Y/N
1	Capital employed is working capital less net equity.	Y/N
2	The working capital cycle is measured in days.	Y/N
3	Commercial papers and bills of exchange are valued in the same way.	Y/N
4	Prices on the money market are affected by the Central Bank.	Y/N
5	LIBID is an average offer rate.	Y/N
6	S/N starts on the day of the transaction.	Y/N
7	On the day of auction of the T-bill, par value is equal to market value.	Y/N
8	Commercial papers require greater disclosure than bills of exchange.	Y/N
9	The central bank financing rate is usually higher than the money market index.	Y/N
10	The credit risk of treasury instruments is always zero.	Y/N

DISCUSSIONS

1. Using the mind map revise the contents of the chapter.
2. Imagine that you are the finance director of an airline. During peak season, you need to gather additional liquidity. Discuss your strategic options.
3. What is the difference between the accounting and controlling view on liquidity?
4. Suppose a subsidiary in your home country has excess liquidity which is dramatically needed for the parent company in your host country. List the methods by which the parent company might make use of the excess liquidity of its subsidiary.
5. Consider how the subprime crisis affected the money market.

SITUATION

PlasticPack Plc

PlasticPack is a public listed company producing packaging for the dairy industry. After a short crash on the market, the company has presently recorded a recovery in sales; however, PlasticPack suffers from liquidity. An extract of PlasticPack's accounts are summarized below:

Profit and loss account for the year ended December 31.

	2016	2017
	€'000	€'000
Sales	13,000	18,000
Cost of sales	7,500	10,100

Operating profit	5,500	7,900
Interests	300	(410)
Profit before tax	5,800	7,490
Tax	(800)	(990)
Profit after tax	5,000	6,500
Dividends	(2,000)	(3,000)
Retained profit	3,000	3,500
Values inside parenthesis indicate that they are negative.		

Balance sheet as of December 31.

	2016		**2017**	
	€'000	€'000	€'000	€'000
Fixed assets		11,000		15,000
Current assets				
Stock	1,000		2,700	
Debtors	1,800		3,300	
Cash	900		200	
Total current assets		3,700		6,200
Total assets		14,700		21,200
Current liabilities				
Overdraft	0		500	
Trade creditors	2,000		2,900	
Other creditors	500		300	
Total current liabilities		(2,500)		(3,700)
Long-term liabilities (loan)		(4,000)		(4,000)
Net assets		8,200		13,500
Ordinary shares (0.5 Euro)		4,000		4,000
Profit and loss and reserves		4,200		9,500
Shareholders' funds		8,200		13,500
Values inside parenthesis indicate that they are negative.				

The bank overdraft cost is 19% p.a.

In order to improve the liquidity position of the company, the treasury manager considers the following scenarios:

1. 3% discount for customers who settle debts within 20 days from the invoice date. It is likely that 50% of existing customers will opt for this.
2. Factor the collection from customers. The expected savings in administration and general expenses would be about €200,000 p.a. and will result in debtor days to be shortened to 30. The factors fee would be 2% of the net sale.

3. Issue the bills of exchange for a nominal value of €400,000 at discount €24,000, payable within 6 months.
4. Issue short-term debenture stock at 13% p.a. pledged with the debtors revenues.

You are required to:

1. Calculate the performance and liquidity ratio based on PlasticPack's account, assess the reason for the liquidity distortion and judge upon the risk that the company is overtrading.
2. State for and against each of the financing strategies and recommend an appropriate policy.

SOLUTION

1. Calculation of the key ratios:
   a. Stock turnover. Because the cost of sale figure is likely to include both fixed and variable costs, a more appropriate calculation of the stock turnover will be in relation to the sales.

	2016	2017
Sales €'000	13,000	18,000
Closing stocks €'000	1,000	2,700
Turnover (days)	28*	55
*(1,000/13,000) × 365		

   b. Current ratio

	2016	2017
Current assets €'000	3,700	6,200
Current liabilities €'000	2,500	3,700
Current ratio	1.48*	1.67
*(3,700/2,500)		

   c. Quick ratio

	2016	2017
Current assets less stock €'000	2,700	3,500
Current liabilities €'000	2,500	3,700
Quick ratio	1.08*	0.94
*(2,700/2,500)		

d. Credit period from suppliers

Similarly as for stock, this will be calculated in relation to sales, as the cost of sales is assumed to be for both fixed and variable costs.

	2016	2017
Sales €'000	13,000	18,000
Closing trade creditors €'000	2,000	2,900
Payment period	56*	59
*(2,000/13,000) × 365		

e. Debt collection period. Because the cost of sale figures are likely to include both fixed and variable costs, a more appropriate calculation of the stock turnover will be in relation to the sales.

	2016	2017
Sales €'000	13,000	18,000
Closing debtors €'000	1,800	3,300
Collection period (days)	51*	67
*(1,800/13,000) × 365		

f. Profitability

	2016		2017	
	€'000	%	€'000	%
Sales	13,000	100	18,000	100
Cost of sales	7,500	58	10,100	56
Operating profit	5,500	42	7,900	44
Interest	300	2	(410)	2
Profit before tax	5,800	45	7,490	42

g. Sale of fixed assets ratio

	2016	2017
Sales €'000	13,000	18,000
Fixed assets €'000	11,000	15,000
Sales of fixed assets	1.18*	1.2
*(1,100/13,000)		

h. Gearing ratio (total debt/total equity)

	2016	2017
	€'000	€'000
Overdraft	0	500
Loan	4,000	4,000
Total debt	4,000	4,500
Ordinary shares	4,000	4,000
Reserves (incl. P&L)	4,200	9,500
Total equity	8,200	13,500
Gearing	49%*	33%
*Total debt to total equity (4,000/8,200) × 100%.		

Conclusion from the performance analysis:

PlasticPack is profitable; the gearing has fallen by 49% since 20 × 16 to 33% in 20 × 17. The net resources (cash plus overdraft) have fallen from €900k to €700k. This reflects mainly the fact of an increase of the stock debtors, and fixed assets, which was partly financed from the increase of the trade creditor. Net assets increased by €5.3 m, which was financed with reserves, as there were no changes to the long-term liabilities.

Although the cash position of the firm has worsened, the overall profitability remains almost unchanged. Operating profit increased slightly from 42% to 44%. A sale to fixed assets remains constant. The creditors' period rose slightly, but the debtors' collection period has significantly worsened from 51 to 67 days. The quick ratio dropped to 0.94, but current ratio improved from 1.48 to 1.67 due to stock.

An overtrading situation occurs when the fixed assets base remains unchanged while sales increase. In the case of PlasticPack, the sales increased together with the assets base, thus, even if the liquidity had worsened, there were no signs of overtrading. PlastickPack is expanding its business. As a result, further finance is required.

2.
   a. The collection period is 67 days. If the discount schema is applied, and 50% of the debtors take part, the debtors' collection will become:

   $(50\% \times 67) + (50\% \times 20) = 43.5$

Thus, the investment to debtors will fall by:

€18 m × 43.5/365 = €2,145k

Savings (assuming financing from overdrafts) would be:

(€3,300k – €2,145k) × 19% = €219.5k

but the cost of the discount would be:

€18 m × 50% × 3% = €270k

Thus, the net benefit would be €50.5k per year (219.5–270).

b. If factoring is applied, the result would be:
Investment to debtors:

€18 m × 30/365 = €1,497k

the saving for financing would be:

(€ 3,300k – €1,497k) × 19% = €342.5k

savings in administration costs would be €200k.

Thus, the total savings of €542.5, offset by the cost of factor fees of €18 m × 2% = €360k, thus the net savings amount to €182.5k.
c. The financing cost would be 24/400 × 2 = 12%, with no reporting requirements.
d. The cost of financing would be 13%; however, the pledge on the assets should be taken into account with reporting requirements.

Conclusion on the Financing Strategies

PlasticPack should factor the receivables and decrease the cost of financing by issuing bills of exchange.

Y/N QUESTIONS' ANSWERS

1	2	3	4	5	6	7	8	9	10
N	Y	Y	Y	N	N	N	Y	Y	N

CHAPTER 8

Fixed Income Instruments

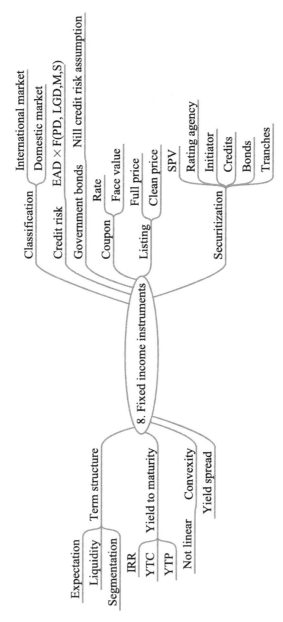

Finance: A Quantitative Introduction. http://dx.doi.org/10.1016/B978-0-12-801584-1.00008-1

8.1 CLASSIFICATION

Typical classification of fixed income instruments:

Types of Fixed Income Instruments	Note
Money market instruments	Discussed in Chapter 7
Obligation (Bonds) market (debentures market)	Discussed in this chapter

The difference between money market and capital market instruments lies with the intention of the investor. On the money market, the primary goal is liquidity and on the capital market it is the return.

A typical capital market fixed income instrument is an obligation (bond). There are also other instruments with variable interest, such as a floating rate obligation, nevertheless, typically the obligation is issued with fixed interest.

Let us examine an obligation of 100 euros nominal value with 5% per annum which is repayable within 5 years. Such an obligation produces the following cash flow:

- An initial payment of (100) euros to purchase the obligation (cash outflow from investor point of view)
- Receipt of 5 euros for 5 consecutive years
- Finally, receipt of 100 euros of capital at the end of 5th year

Such a construction is sensitive to inflation. If during this period, annual inflation was 6%, the obligation would yield a negative real return. For this reason, the majority of debt obligation is now indexed at the premium above inflation, for example, the rate of inflation plus 2%, making the fixed income instruments a bit less fixed (called floating rate).

The bond market globally can be split into the following segments:

- The national bond market
- The international bond market – for example, the Eurobond market

The national bond market can be divided into:

- domestic issuer market
- foreign issuer market

Foreign issuers may issue on the territory of the host country; the obligation may be denominated in the host country currency or in any different currency.

The difference between the foreign issuer market and the Eurobond market lies in the following characteristic of Eurobonds:

- Eurobonds are not registered (with supervisory bodies)
- They are issued outside the jurisdiction of any country
- Usually their underwriter is an international syndicate

The following table represents the classification of Eurobonds:

Issuer	Market	Coupon Rate	Provision Type	Currency	Underlying Assets
Corporate	Primary	Zero-coupon	Call and refunding	Local	ABS
Sovereign	Secondary	Step-up-notes	Prepayments	Foreign	CDO
					CLO
Semigovernment		Deferred Coupon	Sinking Fund		Tax Backed Debts (TBD)
Local Government		Floating-Rate			Revenue Bond
Bank Obligation		Accrued Interest			

Grey shading denotes the most popular bonds in Europe.

Corporate debts can be split into following three broad categories:

- Corporate bonds
- Medium-term notes
- Commercial papers

Corporate bonds are capital market instruments, whereas medium-term notes and commercial papers are associated with the money market. Commercial papers are divided into two groups depending on the placement method, they are either placed directly by issuer or via the dealer.

Corporate debts can be secured, unsecured (also called debentures bonds), or enhanced.

A long-term security that pays interest and capital on redemption is called a bond. Secured bonds are either mortgage debt (secured with real estate or personal property), or collateral trust bonds (secured with financial assets).

Enhanced bonds are guaranteed either by a third party, or by the bank (with a bank letter or credit).

8.2 CREDIT RISK

Generally, credit risk exposure is measured using the following model:

$$\text{Credit risk} = \text{EAD} \times F(\text{PD}, \text{LGD}, \text{M}, \text{S}) \tag{8.1}$$

where:

- EAD is exposure at default, expressing the value of the bonds (credit) at the moment of the debtor default (e.g., bankruptcy announcement)
- F is link function with the following variables:
  - PD = probability of default of the debtor,
  - LGD = loss incurred given default, the fraction of EAD which is to be lost at default,
  - M = maturity of debt obligation, and
  - S = size of the debtor.

Thus, the default rates (what is the chance that a given creditor will not repay his/her obligation) and the recovery rate (what is the amount recovered from the total obligation if debtor has defaulted) are the significant characteristics of the issuer and the specific bond issue. This model is applicable to all debt obligations; however, it is mostly used for corporate bonds.

8.3 GOVERNMENT BONDS

Sovereign bonds are issued by the government (Ministry of Finance, State Treasury, etc.). It is often assumed that these bonds bear insignificant credit risk, so the coupon rate is usually taken to indicate a risk-free rate for the given country. Sovereign bonds are usually distributed at auctions, these can be cyclical and ad hoc auctions. Similar procedures are used for money market and capital market instruments.

There are different names for different government bonds, for example:

- German government bonds are called Bunds (with maturity of 8–30 years) or Bundesobligationen – Bobls (with maturity of 5 years)
- UK – Gilts or "gilt-edged stocks" (hard copy of the bond used to have golden-colored gilded edges)
- France – OATs (Obligation Assimilable du Trèsor) with 2–5 years maturity

- Poland – EOD – with 10 years maturity available only to Polish residents.

A semigovernmental institution may issue bonds too. Examples of such institutions include: GNMA (Ginnie Mae), Federal National Mortgage Association (Fannie Mae), Federal Home Loan Mortgage Corporation (Freddie Mac), Students Loan Marketing Association (Sallie Mae) in the USA or *Fundusz Ochrony Środowiska* in Poland. The agencies issue mortgage-backed securities, asset-backed securities or collateralized mortgage obligations (CMOs).

8.4 COUPON

The coupon rate is the rate the issuer agrees to pay each year; it is the nominal rate. The coupon is the annual amount of the interest payment made to the bondholder. The amount that the issuer agrees to repay the bondholder at the maturity date is called par value. Other words for par value are: maturity value, redemption value, face value, principal value.

The coupon value is established by:

$$Coupon = coupon\,rate \times face\,value \qquad (8.2)$$

Example:

A bond has 7% coupon rate and a face value of 500 euros. The coupon is:

$500 \times 7\% = 35$ euros

The typical reference to the bond is by coupon rate and maturity, for example:

"10s of 21/11/14" indicate the bond of 10% p.a. coupon rate due at November 21, 2014.

Typically, the bond makes interest payments at yearly intervals. There are, however, different typical frequencies for different types of bonds, for example, USA market bonds are payable in two semiannual installments, mortgage-backed securities and asset-backed securities pay interest on a monthly basis.

Bonds which are constructed to not make periodic payments are called *zero-coupon bonds*. These bonds are sold with substantial discount from their par value, and redeemed with face value at their maturity.

Example:

A bond of nominal value of 500 euros is sold on the prime market at 470 euros. If the due date is in 12 months, then the coupon rate is 30/500; this is 6% p.a.

Generally speaking, the value of a fixed income instrument is its discounted cash flow.

$$P = \sum_{t=1}^{n} \frac{C_t}{(1+r)^t} \qquad (8.3)$$

where

C_t = cash flow for the period t,

n = number of years of the investment,

r = required return for investor, and

P = value of the obligation (or price, or amount invested – depending on the purpose).

It should be noted that the formula (8.3) assumes a discrete cash flow and defined time.

There is an assumption that the cash flow would be paid as promised, this means that there is no credit risk present. If there was credit risk, it would be reflected in an enhanced desired return.

Example:

A bond has a nominal value of 100 euros, with 5% coupon, for a 3-year maturity. What is its value if the market rate (investor required return) is equal to 3%?

Solution:

$$P = \frac{100 \times 5\%}{1+3\%} + \frac{100 \times 5\%}{(1+3\%)^2} + \frac{100 \times 5\% + 100}{(1+3\%)^3} = 105.7$$

The required return of the investor is his/her cost of financing (or alternative financing).

A bond with a coupon rate that increases over time is called a step-up note.

Example:

A bond due in 3 years has the following coupon rates: 5% for the first year, 6% for the second year and 7% for the third year.

Deferred coupon bonds are bonds where the interest payments due are deferred for a given number of periods.

Example:

A 100 euro face value bond for 5 years, at 15% deferred two years, will make interest payments 3 times – in years 3, 4, and 5. Note that the coupon rate is significantly higher than that of a bond without a deferred period.

A floating rate coupon is not fixed. It is linked to a changing basis, for example:

- coupon rate = inflation rate plus 3%
- coupon rate = LIBOR plus 2%.

The rate can be subject to a maximum and minimum restriction called a "cap" and a "floor".

Example:

The coupon rate is equal to the inflation rate plus 3% with a cap of 6% and a floor of 4%, thus even if inflation drops to zero, the coupon rate will still be 4%. If inflation increases to 7%, the coupon rate will remain at 6%.

The value of a floating rate bond immediately after coupon payment is equal to its face value.

8.5 LISTING

If the bond holder (seller) sells the bond to an investor (buyer) between the coupon dates, the entire coupon earned for the period will be paid to the buyer. Thus the seller of the bond gives up the interest from the time of the last coupon to the date of sale (period). The amount of interest over this period will be credited to the buyer even if it was earned by the seller and is called the accrued interest (there can be a reverse agreement relating to the accrued interest but such situations are rather exceptional). Thus there are two notations:

- full price (dirty price) – a price with accrued interest
- clean price – a price without accrued interest

so:

$$\text{full price} = \text{clean price} + \text{accrued interest} \qquad (8.4)$$

Note that the quoting of bonds is usually given as the percentage of the nominal value (face value), thus the alternative calculation of the full price will be:

$$\text{full price} = \text{quote of the bond in \% of nominal value} \qquad (8.5)$$
$$\times \text{nominal value} + \text{accrued interest}$$

For interest calculation, an assumption should be taken about the number of days of interest and days during the year. There are the following possible scenarios:

- A year is deemed to have 360 or 365 days or actual according to the calendar used
- A month is 30 days or number of days according to the calendar

Example:

Suppose a bond with semiannual payments of coupon at 5% p.a. coupon rate, with a face value of 10 000 euros. The quoting as of today (15th March) on the stock exchange is 97%. The coupon is payable on June 30 and December 31. Calculate the full and clean price for all days' conventions. The Olympic Games were 2 years before the transaction.

Solution:

The clean price is 97% times the face value 10,000, which equals 9,700 euros.

The dirty price is the clean price of 9700, plus the accrued interest.

Days calculation

Month	30-days	Calendar days
January	30	31
February	30	28
March (15)	15	15
Total	75	74

Coupon is $10,000 \times 5\%$ annually, in two payments (semiannually) of 250 euros (accrued interest: 10,000 @ 5% @ 1/2).

Accrued interest is estimated based on different conventions:

		Calendar/Calendar	Calendar/360	30/Calendar	30/360
Accrued interest basis	A	74/365	74/360	75/365	75/360
Time ratio	B	0.2027	0.2056	0.2055	0.2083
Accrued interest	$250 \times B$	50.675	51.4	51.375	52.075
Full price 9700+accrued interest		**9750.675**	**9751.4**	**9751.375**	**9752.075**

While holding a bond, the market situation can change. Suppose an issuer issued bonds with a fixed 8% coupon rate when the market rate was 5%, if the market rate drops to 2%, the issuer will still be obligated to pay the 8% face value. Therefore, some issuers reserve the right to redeem the issue sooner, that is, before bond maturity; this is called a "call provision."

Usually the call provision is deferred in time, for example, 8-year bonds may be called back after only 3 years. In such a situation, the 3-year period is call the deferral period.

Call provision can be executed on the entire issue or on part of the bonds, which are usually randomly picked up. The redemption price for the call provision can be fixed in advance, based on any formula defined by the issuer or based on the market conditions.

Bonds with the option to be repaid before maturity, i.e., with call provision, are called callable bonds. If a bond has no protection against early call then it is referred to as a "currently callable bond".

A weaker form than call protection is a fund protection. In contrast to call protection, fund protection prevents redemption from specific funds only (usually other debts issue).

A reverse right to call provision is the right for the bondholder to ask for early redemption, called a "put provision".

The call and put provisions are examples of embedded options into a bond contract. This is important for accounting purposes as the embedded option can be valued separately from the main instruments, and disclosed separately from the main instruments, provided they are tradable.

Prepayment on coupon is virtually identical to a call option; however, it denotes an overpayment of the capital liability part of the bond.

To reduce the credit risk attached to the issue, an amortization schedule is produced for the issue to be repaid before maturity. In such a situation, a portion of the issue is repaid early every year. Another credit risk management tool is the "conversion option", which allows converting the bonds into equity.

The bond is usually denominated in the currency of the issuer (i.e., a company with its seat in the UK will issue bonds in pounds, in Australia, Australian Dollars, in Czech Republic, Czech Crowns, etc.); however, it can be denominated in other currencies too. It is also possible to denominate capital in one currency and the coupon in another.

8.6 SECURITIZATION

Similarly to loans, bonds can be backed up by assets, rights or guaranties. Typical bonds can be securitized with mortgage loans. Thus, the repayment of the bond is linked to the repayments of the loans. The securitization process allows entering the primary assets (loan which is not offered to the secondary market) into secondary markets.

The typical mechanism is as follows:

A bank or agency gathers a pool of mortgage loans (say, 10,000 credit agreements).

Because of bank law and confidentiality, a transfer of the loan receivable will also mean a transfer of confidential information about the loan (incomes, occupation, personal data, assurance, pledges, other assets, etc.); thus, if the bank issues a bond instead, it does not have to reveal the confidential information. As there are a significant number of loans, the characteristic of a single loan is not significant to the entire portfolio of loans. Thus, instead of revealing information on a single loan, the bank presents statistical information on the entire portfolio of loans. For example, what is the probability of default in this portfolio, what is the recovery rate, amount due at default, payment schedule, and so on? To issue the bonds, the bank defines the portfolio, describes it, and puts it as the backup asset for investors in bonds.

The securitization procedure described above has the following drawbacks:

1. It replicates the population risk profile to the securities issued.

2. If the bank has financial problems, then the credit risk is increased, thus the investor would add a premium above the portfolio risk to compensate for the inherent risk of the bank.

To sort out these drawbacks, the following amendments to the procedure are used on the market.

1. The portfolio of loans can be divided into tranches with different risk profiles, and different classes of bonds can be sold to investors with different attitudes to risk.
2. An independent party sets up a new company (called a Special Purpose Vehicle or SPV) without the credit risk of the initiator (bank). Then the initiator will transfer all rights related to the selected loans to the SPV and based on this contract, the SPV will issue bonds without the initiator credit risk premium.

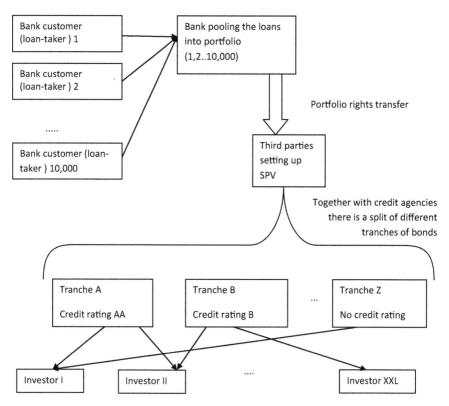

Basic securitization scheme

A similar structure can be established with different classes of assets, for example, car loans, consumer loans, credit cards, and commercial assets loans (trade receivables, ships, etc.). In such situation, bonds are called asset-backed securities (ABS). A subgroup of ABS is obligations which are backed up with a portfolio of a different class of assets, for example, a combination of corporate loans, receivables with emerging markets bonds, or foreign bank loans. Such bonds are known as collateralized debt obligation (CDO). If the portfolio of collateralized asset is combined only with different types of bank loans, such as securities, then they are denoted as collateralized loan obligation (CLO).

Active participation of the credit rating provider is needed in order to structure an ABS or CDO. Because the SPV balance sheet is clean, the fundamental analysis of risk and asset performance stays with bank assets, thus it becomes vague and sensitive in terms of reporting and independent data access. There are also doubts in treatment (exclusion) of the portfolio from the balance sheet of the bank, unless virtually all significant risk and profits are transferred to the SPV.

Another motivation for securitization is capital requirements and the tax system recognition of taxable losses. Usually, the tax system does not allow recognition of the provision of losses on underperforming loans, unless formal legal action is undertaken against the debtor or the assets are sold. The transfer of rights to an SPV is usually recognized as a tax-deductable cost, thus allowing the bank to recognize the losses without accepting the formal costs of loan recovery. The SPV scheme also allows a decrease of the regulatory capital requirement, which is a motive for the capital supervision of the bank.

Taxed-backed debt obligations are instruments issued by states, countries, districts, cities, or other regions backed with some form of tax revenue.

Revenue bonds are issued for financing and are backed up with revenues from defined projects.

Similarly to the equity market, we differentiate a primary and secondary bond market.

8.7 TERM STRUCTURE

The price of money is the interest rate, consequently the cost of the bond to the issuer is the coupon rate.

The basis for the price of bonds and price of shares differs fundamentally.

Example:

A company, ABC plc, has issued 2,000,000 ordinary shares, which are listed on a recognized stock exchange at 2 euros per share. At the same time, ABC plc issues the following bonds series as of today:

Bond Name	Quantity	Nominal Value per Share	Coupon Rate (per Annum)	Years to Maturity	Coupon Payments Every
ABC 1 year	2,000,000	100	2%	1	Year
ABC 2 years	2,000,000	100	2.2%	2	Year
ABC 3 years	2,000,000	100	2.6%	3	Year
ABC 4 years	2,000,000	100	2.7%	4	Year

All of the above bond issues are similar in terms of the bond characteristics, except for the coupon rate and maturity.

Technically, ABC plc might issue only shares which are ordinary shares and each issue of shares will have characteristics similar to the previous issue. The next issue of 1,000,000 ordinary shares could be added to the existing pool of shares. As regards bonds, the company might issue different types of bonds in terms of maturity, thus we cannot quote one year and two year maturity papers the same. This is the reason why the specific issue of bonds with maturity is used, while the ordinary shares are treated homogeneously. Thus, the rating may differ for shares and specific issue of bonds, even for the same company (issuer).

By drawing a chart showing years to maturity and the coupon rate, we obtain a curve called the structure of interest (in our case, nominal coupon) rates for ABC plc.

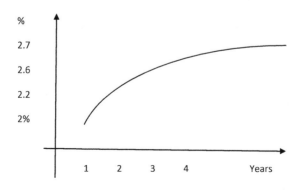

This shape of curve is "classical" (or normal), meaning that the longer the investment horizon, the higher the credit risk and frozen capital and, therefore, the required income for an investor is higher. The actual curve can have different shapes, for example:

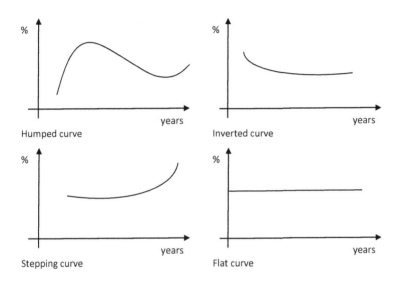

We would obtain similar types of shape if, instead of the coupon rate, we were to apply the return rate.

The shape of the term structure can be explained with three basic theories:

- expectation theory
- liquidity premium theory and
- market segmentation

Expectation theory on an example states that the return of 2 years' bond is equal to the return in the current year plus the expected return for the bond purchased in one year's time. Thus it shows the expectation of the market. If the 1 year return is 5% and the six year return is 6%, this means that the short-term 1 year interest rate is going to increase in the future. Thus, the shape of the term structure shows investor expectation on short-term rate behavior. This theory assumes, however, that investors are indifferent to risk factors (such as interest rate, maturity, credit risk, etc.).

Liquidity premium theory states that the longer the maturity, the higher the liquidity risk. Thus the rate is increased to the liquidity premium. The shape of the curve is subject to two factors; one is expectation and the second is the risk premium for liquidity. This theory is also known as "biased expectation theory."

Market segmentation is the basic idea that each maturity sector is independent. This is because different investors have different return needs. Basically, there are two types of investors; those who manage funds against a benchmark (e.g., the bond market index) and those who manage funds against their liabilities. An example of investors in the first group is mutual funds, whereas for the second group, the industry companies. An investor who matches the maturity to the liabilities will select the sector of maturities which best reflects his liabilities (basic principle of asset-liability matching), thus he will not be interested in other sectors of maturity. The conclusion of the theory is that any shape of curve is possible.

The curve showing the interest terms may move in time in the following ways:

- shift – the returns go up or down
- twist – a change of slope
- butterfly – the shape changes

We discussed the idea of the term structure based on the simple example of ABC plc. However, there were hidden assumptions in our example: (i) we assumed that the issue of bonds is on the same date (i.e., today) and (ii) that ABC plc has negligible credit risk. Let us relax those assumptions. The first relaxation will be on the coupon rate and actual return on the bond. We will introduce the concept of yield to maturity (YTM).

8.8 YIELD TO MATURITY

Until now, we have considered the primary bonds market. The return to the investor was approximated by the coupon rate. On the secondary market, the investor can buy the bond above or below its par value (we refer to the clean price), thus the actual return is different to that promised by the issuer.

Example:

WXZ plc issues a debenture for 5 years, with interest payable every December 31, at yearly intervals at the coupon rate of 5%. The face value of the bond is 1000 euros. Consider (i) what was the value of the bond at issue to the investor whose required rate of return equals 4%, (ii) if the investor bought the bond for 978 euros (clean) at December 31 of the second year, what should the interest rate be?

Solution:

By application of the formula:

$$P = \sum_{t=1}^{n} \frac{C_t}{(1+r)^t}$$

we arrive at:

$$P = \frac{1,000 \times 5\%}{1+4\%} + \frac{1,000 \times 5\%}{(1+4\%)^2} + \frac{1,000 \times 5\%}{(1+4\%)^3} + \frac{1,000 \times 5\%}{(1+4\%)^4} \qquad \text{(i)}$$
$$+ \frac{1,000 \times 5\% + 1,000}{(1+4\%)^5} = 1,044.5$$

$$978 = \sum_{t=1}^{n} \frac{C_t}{(1+r)^t} \qquad \text{(ii)}$$

Thus:

$$978 = \frac{1,000 \times 5\%}{1+\text{Return}} + \frac{1,000 \times 5\%}{(1+\text{Return})^2} + \frac{1,000 \times 5\% + 1,000}{(1+\text{Return})^3}$$

In this case, the return required to balance the equation is unknown. The solution to this equation is found using trial and error and the return is found to be 5.82%. Note that the calculated return is in fact the internal rate of return (IRR) but is called in this instance the YTM.

To conclude, in order to measure the return on the bond bought on a secondary market, we need to calculate the IRR of the bond's cash flow stream. This IRR is called YTM. This is in addition to the indicator of the current cost of debt to the issuer. The assumption behind YTM is similar to that of IRR, in that the investor will be able to reinvest interest at the YTR rate. If not, the investor will be exposed to interest rate risk. The formula for the YTM calculation is as follows:

$$\text{Amount invested} = \sum_{t=1}^{n} \frac{C_t}{(1+YTM)^t} \qquad (8.6)$$

The YTM calculated for bonds, which pay interest more frequently than on a yearly basis, is called "Bond Equivalent Yield".

The YTM concept assumes slight changes in the case of putable or callable bonds, if their maturity moment is on a flexible basis, at the discretion of either the investor or issuer. Thus, the YTM changes into yield to call (YTC) and yield to put (YTP). As a matter of standard, the YTC and YTP are equal to YTM calculated to the earliest moment of possibility to execute the option.

Example:

An investor holds two recently purchased bonds: (i) a callable bond of 500 nominal value with 2% coupon bought at 498, which is a 10-year bond with 2 years' deferral from now, and (ii) a putable bond of 200 nominal value with 3% coupon bought at 201 with 5 years' maturity and 1 year deferral from now. Calculate the YTC and YTP, respectively.

Solution:

	Callable	Putable
Formula	$498 = \dfrac{500 \times 2\%}{1+YTC} + \dfrac{500 \times 2\% + 500}{(1+YTC)^2}$	$201 = \dfrac{200 \times 3\% + 200}{(1+YTP)^1}$
Value	YTC = 2.2074%	YTP = 2.7389%

The yield for the zero-coupon bond is calculated as the effective rate – this is the geometric average of future values and amount invested (or price)

$$YTM = \sqrt[n]{\frac{\text{Future value}}{\text{Amount invested}}} - 1 \qquad (8.7)$$

The yield of the zero-coupon bond is called the spot rate. The yield of the zero-coupon Treasury bond is called the Treasury spot rate. Thus, the relation between maturity and Treasury spot rate is called the term structure of interest rate (the credit risk is negligible).

The simplicity of the abovestated formula makes it popular for establishing the term structure curve based on zero-coupon securities. Another argument for its application is the lack of reinvestment risk.

The amount invested is the price of the bond paid by the bondholder – it could be on the primary market – nominal value, or the secondary market – market value. Therefore, in order to define the term structure, we may use the return measured as the YTM instead of the coupon rate.

Example:

A zero-coupon bond of nominal value 340 and current market price 328 matures in 7 years. What is the YTM?

Solution:

$$\text{YTM} = \sqrt[7]{\frac{340}{329}} - 1 = 0.5\%$$

8.9 CONVEXITY

The equation for zero-coupon YTM shows the relation between YTM and the amount invested (price of the bond). Such a relation is not linear. For fixed coupon bonds, the future price changes with the time remaining to maturity. The amount invested reflects market prices at the moment of investment, and YTM benchmarks the investor return. Thus, only by drawing the relation price (amount invested) to YTM might we observe some characteristics of bonds.

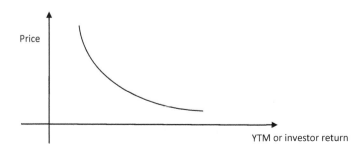

The graph shows the adverse relation between the price and investor return or the market rates. As rates increase in economies, prices become lower (we assume a fixed coupon bond). Secondly, the graph indicates that movements of YTM up or down do not result in a movement in price of the same proportion. This characteristic is known as convexity.

Convexity is different for different bonds.

Coupon and YTM are interest rates offered either by the issuer or calculated by the investor based on the price-return conditions. In the economy, interest rates are generally recognized as the cost of money. The money itself is "produced" by the central bank (monetary base) and subsequently distributed by the banking system, via the monetary multiplier and of course by foreign entities exchanging local currency for foreign currency. These factors together impact the demand and supply of money, which is a subject of macroeconomic research. On the other hand, the central bank influences the money market by making the open market operation possible and applying other macroeconomic tools. In consequence, there are indexes set up on the money market (e.g., LIBOR), which reflect the average cost of the money in the economy in terms of a percentage rate. The term structure of any company's bonds will not be equal to the general behavior of the market because of:

- credit risk
- size of the issue (popularity on the market)

The term structured curve is derived based on the sovereign bonds (government bonds) in order to eliminate credit and size bias risk.

8.10 YIELD SPREAD

Since sovereign bonds are deemed to be risk-free, any other market players should offer for the same maturity issue and the yield offered on the sovereign bonds and risk credit premium.

The definition of yield spread is:

$$\text{Yield spread} = \text{yield on bond A less yield on bond B} \qquad (8.8)$$

Yield spread can be denoted as absolute yield spread, where bond B is the reference bond (e.g., Treasury bond) and bond A is the measured bond.

The yield can be measured in different ways and the formulas are given below:

$$\text{Relative yield spread} = \frac{\text{yield on bond A} - \text{yield on bond B}}{\text{yield on bond B}} \quad (8.9)$$

$$\text{Yield ratio} = \frac{\text{yield on bond A}}{\text{yield on bond B}} \quad (8.10)$$

$$\text{After-tax yield} = \text{Pre-tax yield} \times (1 - \text{marginal tax rate}) \quad (8.11)$$

$$\text{Taxable equivalent yield} = \frac{\text{tax} - \text{exempt yield}}{(1 - \text{marginal tax rate})} \quad (8.12)$$

Example:

As of today, 5 year Treasury bonds' YTM is 5.32%, whereas 5 year GMR plc bonds YTM is 5.77%. Assuming the investor-effective tax rate to be 33%, what are the yield spreads and after-tax yield on GMR bonds, what would it change to if GRM bonds were to yield 5% tax-exempt yield?

Solution:

	Formula	Value
Absolute yield spread	5.77 − 5.32	0.45%
Relative yield spread	$\dfrac{5.77 - 5.32}{5.32}$	8.45%
Yield ratio	$\dfrac{5.77}{5.32}$	1.085
After-tax yield	5.77 × (1 − 0.33)	3.87%
Taxable equivalent yield	$\dfrac{5\%}{(1 - 0.33)}$	7.5%

The yield spread between non-Treasury and Treasury securities that are the same in all respects except for credit rating which is also called the "credit spread". It is believed that the credit spread is an indicator for the business cycle – during an economic downturn, it becomes larger, whereas during economic expansion, it becomes smaller.

8.11 SUMMARY

Fixed income instruments are traded on both the money and capital markets. A typical capital instrument is an obligation (or bond). The bond market is divided into national and international markets. On the national (domestic market), bonds can be denominated in national currency as well as in foreign currency. The bonds market can be defined according to issuer, the market itself, coupon rate, provisions, currency, and back-up asset.

The bond significant risk factor is default of the issuer, credit risk is assessed by the credit rating institution or with the application of models. Sovereign (treasury) bonds are traded as credit risk-free instruments; this is, however, an assumption.

Bonds yield coupon. The coupon of the bond might be fixed or floating. An interest may be payable by the issuer during the life of the bond. The price of the bond can be provided with interest (full-price) or ex-interest (clean or naked price). A zero-coupon bond does not pay interest during the life of the instrument. The accrued interest can be calculated based on different assumptions with regard to the number of days to maturity and total number of days during the year.

The difference between a bond and a loan is that the loan does not have a secondary market. One of the methods of releasing liquidity from a loan is a securitization. It is generally a "repackaging" of existing assets (loans) into securities of different risk and return profiles.

The relation between maturity and price of the bond is called a term structure of the interest rates. This is not a linear relation. It is characterized by convexity. There is no single universal explanation of the term structure of rates.

The YTM is the internal rate of return of the bond's cash flow. It is the basic method for the cost of debt assessment. Credit risk might be assessed by analyzing the yield difference between zero credit risk sovereign bonds and the examined bond.

FURTHER READING

An explanation of the bank role in securitization including enhancement is provided by B. Mandel et al. (Mandel, Morgan, & Wei, 2012).

Contingent capital certificate as a risk management tool is shown in M. Flannery paper (Flannery, 2010)

Y/N QUESTIONS

Number	Question	Y/N
1	A bond issued at coupon 2% + inflation is a floating rate bond.	Y/N
2	EAD is expressed in money.	Y/N
3	EOS is a kind of the ABS.	Y/N
4	Zero coupon bonds pay dividend.	Y/N
5	Clean price is equal to full price less accumulated earnings.	Y/N
6	Securitization involves a vehicle company which is owned by initiator.	Y/N
7	YTM is equal to IRR.	Y/N
8	YTC is equal to YTP.	Y/N
9	The value of a floating rate bond after coupon payment is equal to nominal value.	Y/N
10	On a 360 day base, February has 30 days.	Y/N

DISCUSSIONS

1. Using the mind map revise the content of the chapter.
2. The value of a fixed income is established based on the formula

   $P = \sum_{t=1}^{n} \dfrac{C_t}{(1+r)^t}$ – explains the assumption behind it and discuss the

   difference between return and coupon rate used in it.
3. Explain the role of the credit rating agency in securitization scheme.
4. As of today, a 6 year Treasury bond's YTM is 6.31% while a 6 year GMR plc bond's YTM is 6.83%. Assuming the investor effective tax rate to be 23%, what are the yield spreads and after-tax yield on GMR bonds, to what would it change if GRM bonds were to yield 4% tax-exempt yield?
5. Compare the acronyms used for the treasury bonds in your home and host countries.

SITUATION

Anna Maria plc (AM) is a Romanian company listed on the stock exchange. AM is involved in the seed production (agriculture). The company operates on the Central European market. The company has a good track record of market success.

The capital structure of AM plc is as follows:

Equity		€m	€m
	Ordinary shares (par value €1 per share)	70	
	Reserves	35	
			105
Debt			
	Bond Factory (par value €100) @ 8.9%	20	
	Bond R&D (par value €200) @ 8%	15	
			35
			140

Bond factory has been issued to finance a new production plant.

Bond factory will be redeemed at par in 10 years' time and pays annual interest of 8.9%. The current ex-interest market price of the bond is €96.03.

Bond R&D will be redeemed at par in 4 years' time and pays annual interest of 8.4%. The cost of debt of this bond is 8.12% per year. The current ex-interest market price of the bond is €102.01.

Both bonds were issued at the same time. Ignore taxation.

You are required to:

1. Calculate the cost of debt of Bond Factory.
2. Discuss the reasons why different bonds of the same company might have different costs of debt.

SOLUTION

a. The cost of debt of Bond Factory is the YTM (IRR) at current conditions. It can be found by linear interpolation.

Using 10%, the difference between the present value of future cash flows and the ex-interest market value

$$= \sum_{t=1}^{10} 8.9 \times (1.10)^{-t} + (100 \times \frac{1}{(1.10)^{10}}) - 96.03 = (€\,2.78).$$

Since the net present value is negative, 10% is higher than the cost of debt.

Using 9%, the difference between the present value of future cash flows and the ex-interest market value

$$= \sum_{t=1}^{10} 8.9 \text{ x } (1.09)^{-t} + (100 \times \frac{1}{(1.09)^{10}}) - 96.03 = € 3.32.$$

As the net present value is positive, 9% is lower than the cost of debt.

Cost of bond factory
    = 9 + ((10 − 9) x 3.32)/(3.32 + 2.78) = 9 + 0.29 = 9.29%.

9.29% is an approximation of the cost of debt for Bond Factory (the differences in true value – 9.534% – arising due to linearity of the method).

Typically, the longer the time to maturity of a debt, the higher will be the interest rate and the cost of debt. Bond factory has the greater time to maturity and therefore would be expected to have a higher interest rate compared to the Bond R&D.

Liquidity preference theory suggests that investors require compensation for postponing consumption. Lending for longer periods makes default risk increase with time.

Expectations theory suggests that the shape of the yield curve depends on the investors' expectations as to future interest rates. If the expectation is that future interest rates will be higher than current interest rates, the yield curve will slope up.

Market segmentation theory suggests that future interest rates depend on conditions in different debt markets such as the short-term market, the medium-term market and the long-term market. The shape of the yield curve therefore depends on the supply of, and demand for, funds in the market segments.

Because both bonds were issued at the same time by AM plc, the business risk of MM plc can be discounted for as a reason for the difference between the two costs of debt. Part of this risk will be associated with the credit risk due to mismatch of maturities between Factory and R&D bond.

In case of small and not liquid markets, the size of the issue may also impact the costs of debt. The bigger the issue, the lower the costs.

Y/N QUESTIONS' ANSWERS

1	2	3	4	5	6	7	8	9	10
Y	Y	N	N	N	N	Y	N	Y	Y

APPENDIX A

Time Value of Money

Suppose that you currently have 100 euros (Year 0). Your bank offers you a deposit rate of 4.3% per annum. What would be the future value of your deposit if you decide to put your capital into the account?

Its value at year 1 (1 year into the future) will be:

$$100 + 100 \times 4.3\% = 100 + 4.3 = 104.3.$$

Suppose that in year 1 the bank offered you a rate of 5% per annum. What will be the value after 2 years? This would depend on your strategy because after year 1, you already have 100 euros of your original capital and 4.3 euros of your capital gain, that is, interest received, so you might reinvest only the capital, only the interest, or both. In each case, between year 1 and year 2 you would earn:

1. If you were to invest only the capital, this would mean: 100 + 100 × 5% = 100 + 5 = 105.
2. If you were to invest the capital plus the interest earned in year 1, then: 104.3 + 104.3 × 5% = 104.3 + 5.215 = 109.515.
3. If you were to reinvest only the interest earned in year 1, then 4.3 + 4.3 × 5% = 4.515.

Case 1 shows the simple interest strategy, case 2 shows the compound strategy, and case 3 shows the effect of the reinvestment of interest.

Suppose your bank offered to you 4.3% per annum. In a year's time, you have to pay 100 euros. How much does your initial deposit need to be in order to have 100 euros at the end of year 1? Assume that X is the unknown amount of initial deposit, so:

$X + X \times 4.3\% = 100$, by rearranging the equation we find:

$$X(1 + 0.043) = 100 \text{ thus } X = \frac{100}{(1 + 0.043)} = 95.87.$$

Note that our result is not the difference between the interest earned and the deposit from the example 1.1 (100 − 4.3 = 95.7).

Finance: A Quantitative Introduction. http://dx.doi.org/10.1016/B978-0-12-801584-1.00017-2

Let us extend the question saying that you will need to pay your 100 euros not in 1 year's time, but in 2 years' time, whereas in the second year, the interest rate is 5%. Once again, the answer depends on your investment strategy.

1. If you do not reinvest your interest, your equation will look like this:

$$X + X \times 4.3\% + X \times 4.3\% = 100$$

$$X(1+2\times4.3\%) = 100 \text{ thus } X = \frac{100}{(1+2\times0.043)} = 92.08$$

2. But, if you decide to reinvest both the capital and the interest earned, then the equation will change as follows:

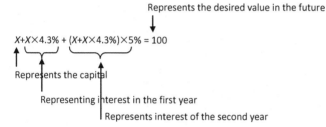

By rearranging the equation, we obtain the following formula:

$$X = 100 \times \frac{1}{(1+0.043)\times(1+0.043)} = 91.92$$

Note that the value of the initial investment necessary for the simple interest (92.08) is higher than the compounded interest (91.92). Why?

Let us introduce the following notation:

i = Interest rate per annum
n = Number of years
E = Expected value (or future value FV)
D = Initial deposit (or present value PV)

Following assumptions can be made:

1. The interest rate remains constant during the years in question
2. Interest earned can be reinvested at the rate i
3. We do not consider taxation and inflation

By making the aforementioned assumptions, it is possible now to provide the formula for both future values and present values as follows:

	Future Value	Present Value
Simple interest	$E = D \times (1 + ni)$	$D = E \times (1 + ni)^{-1}$
Compounded interest	$E = D \times (1 + i)^n$	$D = E \times \dfrac{1}{(1+i)^n}$

The formula $\dfrac{1}{(1+i)^n}$ is called the discount factor.

Consider:

Does i represent a nominal or real interest rate?

If an amount D is invested for n years at the interest rate of i per annum, and the rate is compounded once per annum, the future (terminal) value of the investment is:

$$D(1+i)^n \tag{A1.1}$$

It is possible to approximate the number of years it takes for D to double in value (doubling time) or triple in value (tripling time). The formula is as follows:

$$\text{Doubling time} = \frac{72}{i\%}$$

$$\text{Tripling time} = \frac{110}{i\%}$$

Example:

How many years will it take for a deposit to double and triple in value if the interest rate is 7%?

Solution:

$$\text{Doubling time} = \frac{72}{7} = 10.3 \text{ years}$$

$$\text{Check } 100 \times (1 + 0.07)^{10.3} = 201$$

$$\text{Triple} = \frac{110}{7} = 15.7 \text{ years}$$

However, if the investment is compounded m times a year, the value of the investments changes to:

$$D\left(1+\frac{i}{m}\right)^{mn} \qquad (A1.2)$$

Example:

Consider the changes to the future value of the deposit of 100 euros invested at 5% for 1 year, when the capitalization is yearly, semiyearly, quarterly, and monthly.

Solution:

At $i = 5\%$, $D = 100$

	Yearly	Semiyearly	Quarterly	Monthly
Frequency (m)	1	2	4	12
Period of deposit in years (n)	1	1	1	1
$D\left(1+\dfrac{i}{m}\right)^{mn}$	$100\left(1+\dfrac{0.05}{1}\right)^{1\times1}$	$100\left(1+\dfrac{0.05}{2}\right)^{1\times2}$	$100\left(1+\dfrac{0.05}{4}\right)^{1\times4}$	$100\left(1+\dfrac{0.05}{12}\right)^{1\times12}$
E	105	105.0625	105.0945	105.1162

The future value of long-lasting deposits is sensitive to small changes in the interest rate.

Consider the following situation. A deposit of 1,000 euros is put in a bank account for 40 years at 5% per annum. Its future value would be:

$$FV = 1000 \times (1+0.05)^{40} = 7{,}040 \text{ euros}$$

But if the rate changes to 5.5% (by 10%) the value of the deposit changes to:

$$FV = 1000 \times (1+0.055)^{40} = 8{,}513 \text{ euros}$$

This is $(8{,}513 - 7{,}040)/7{,}040 \times 100\% = 21\%$. A 10% change in the interest rate results in a 21% change in the deposit value.

This is an example of nonlinear relation between changes in the rate of interest and the future value of the deposit. The prices of financial instruments are sensitive to small changes in interest rates in the economy.

If the capital is compounded several times in a year, the present value formula changes as follows:

$$D = E \times \frac{1}{\left(1 + \dfrac{i}{m}\right)^{nm}} \qquad (A1.3)$$

Example:

The bank offers you a monthly capitalization of a deposit at 7% p.a. Your investment period is 4 years. What is the amount of initial investment that you need to put aside to be able to pay a 200 euro bill after the deposit expires?

Solution:

$$D = E \times \frac{1}{\left(1 + \dfrac{i}{m}\right)^{nm}} = 200 \times \frac{1}{\left(1 + \dfrac{0.07i}{12}\right)^{4 \times 12}} = 46.629$$

But what happens if the bank offers a continuous capitalization (it calculates interest with every movement of time)?

The effect of continuous capitalization is that the capital is increased often by a very small amount of interest, thus the capital is accumulating itself. Nevertheless, the increase of the interest due to the increase of the capitalization frequency is limited.

From a mathematical perspective, the limit of the increase of interest is:

$$\lim_{m \to \infty} D \left(1 + \frac{i}{m}\right)^{nm} = De^{in} \qquad (A1.4)$$

For the future value of 1 euro deposit:

$$\lim_{m \to \infty} \left(1 + \frac{i}{m}\right)^{nm} = e^{in} \qquad (A1.5)$$

The present value discount factor is thus e^{-in}, where e – is a constant value of 2.71 (the limit of continuous capitalization).

Example:

You invest 140 euros for 3 years at 5% continuous. What is the future value?

Solution:

$$140 \times e^{0.05 \times 3} = 162$$

Example:

You make an investment of value X at a continuous rate of 4%. At the end of a 6-year investment period, you receive 721 euros. What was the initial amount of money X that you have put into the account?

Solution:

$$721 \times e^{-0.04 \times 6} = 567$$

There is a mathematical relationship between continuous compounded rate and the rate compounded m times per annum.

Suppose i_c represents the continuous compounded rate and i_m the rate compounded m times a year. The following equation holds true:

$$De^{i_c n} = D\left(1 + \frac{i_m}{m}\right)^{nm} \tag{A1.6}$$

After simplification:

$$e^{i_c} = \left(1 + \frac{i_m}{m}\right)^{m} \tag{A1.7}$$

Note that if $y = \ln(x)$ then $x = e^x$. Ln is the natural logarithm function thus:

$$i_c = m \times \ln\left(1 + \frac{i_m}{m}\right) \tag{A1.8}$$

And:

$$i_m = m(e^{\frac{i_c}{m}} - 1)$$ (A1.9)

Example:

The bank offers an interest rate of 8% on deposit with quarterly compounding. In addition to this, it offers a rate of 7.95% for continuous compounding. Which deposit is more favorable for the client?

Solution:

$$i_c = m \times \ln\left(1 + \frac{i_m}{m}\right) = 4\ln(1 + 0.08/4) = 4\ln(1.02) = 7.921.$$ A continuous deposit will be more favorable.

The relationship between different frequencies can be expressed mathematically.

Suppose that a bank offers the rate with frequency m_1, what would be the equivalent rate with frequency m_2? By applying a concept similar to that shown above, we obtain:

$$D\left(1 + \frac{i_{m_1}}{m_1}\right)^{nm_1} = D\left(1 + \frac{i_{m_2}}{m_2}\right)^{nm_2}$$ (A1.10)

So by rearranging:

$$i_{m_2} = \left[\left(1 + \frac{i_{m_1}}{m_1}\right)^{m_1/m_2} - 1\right]m_2$$ (A1.11)

Up to now, we have considered a one-off payment (the initial deposit) and its future or present value. Let us consider a situation when the same amount of money is payable to you at discrete intervals (e.g., yearly). This stream of payments is called an annuity.

Example:

Mr. X decided to pay his daughter 1,000 euros per year for 5 years, starting from now. What is the future value of the payments if the interest rate is 10% per annum?

Solution:

Year	Action	Formula	Value	Cumulative Value
Now	The daughter receives 1,000 and puts it into a bank account for 5 years	FV = 1,000 × (1 + 0.1)⁵	1,610	1,610
End of year 1	The daughter receives 1,000 and puts it into a bank account for 4 years	FV = 1,000 × (1 + 0.1)⁴	1,464	3,074
End of year 2	The daughter receives 1,000 and puts it into a bank account for 3 years	FV = 1,000 × (1 + 0.1)³	1,331	4,405
End of year 3	The daughter receives 1,000 and puts it into bank account for 2 years	FV = 1,000 × (1 + 0.1)²	1,210	5,615
End of year 4	The daughter receives 1,000 and puts it into bank account for 1 years	FV = 1,000 × (1 + 0.1)¹	1,100	6,715

The future value of the annuity is 6,715. The mathematical solution of this would be as follows:

$$FV = 1,000 \times (1+0.1)^5 + 1,000 \times (1+0.1)^4 + 1,000 \times (1+0.1)^3 + 1,000 \times (1+0.1)^2 + 1,000 \times (1+0.1)^1$$

By rearranging the equation, we get:

$$FV = 1,000 \times (1.1^5 + 1.1^4 + \ldots + 1.1)$$

The expression $(1.1^5 + 1.1^4 + \ldots + 1.1)$ is called the annuity factor and is usually tabularized for various periods and interest rates. The annuity factor describes the value of 1 euro payments for a given period at a given rate.

The annuity can be paid all at once. This is called an immediate annuity (annuity due), or it can be paid in arrears (after a year), when it is called an ordinary annuity. In both cases, the number of payments remains unchanged; however, there is a shift in time.

Thus, an immediate annuity would have an FV_{imm} equal to that on the ordinary annuity but multiplied by $1 + i$.

$$FV_{imm} = FV_{ord} \times (1+i) \tag{A1.12}$$

Therefore:

$$FV_{ord} = \frac{FV_{imm}}{(1+i)} \tag{A1.13}$$

The present value of the annuity is similar to discounting:

By referring to the example above, the present value of the cash flow would be as follows:

$$PV = \frac{1,000}{1.1^1} + \frac{1,000}{1.1^2} + \frac{1,000}{1.1^3} + \frac{1,000}{1.1^4} + \frac{1,000}{1.1^5}$$

$$\text{thus by rearranging} = 1,000 \times \left(\frac{1}{1.1^1} + \frac{1}{1.1^2} + \frac{1}{1.1^3} + \frac{1}{1.1^4} + \frac{1}{1.1^5} \right)$$

The fraction $\left(\frac{1}{1.1^1} + \frac{1}{1.1^2} + \frac{1}{1.1^3} + \frac{1}{1.1^4} + \frac{1}{1.1^5} \right)$ is called a discount factor.

An annuity that never ends is called a perpetuity. A perpetuity is a stream of cash flows that lasts forever. An example of a perpetuity is a preferred stock that pays a fixed cash dividend each year. The future value of the perpetuity of 1 euro cannot be calculated as an annuity because the cash stream is infinite. The analytical formula is the limit of the sum of the series:

$$\lim_{m \to \infty} \sum_{n=1}^{\infty} \frac{1}{(1+i)^n} = \frac{1}{i} \qquad (A1.14)$$

An annuity that ends at the time of death of the receiver is called a life-time annuity.

A lifetime annuity is based on the mortality table (also called a life table). The basic mortality table consists of five columns as given in the following table.

Mortality table at age X cumulated (extract)

Age	Number of Survivors	Number of Deceased	Probability of Surviving	Probability of Dying
X	l_x	d_x	p_x	q_x
			$p_x = 1 - q_x$	d_x/l_x
0	100,000	2,392	0.97608	0.02392
10	97,037	32	0.9996702	0.0003298
20	96,375	138	0.9985681	0.0014319
30	94,612	207	0.9978121	0.0021879
40	91,801	414	0.9954902	0.0045098
50	85,896	880	0.9897551	0.0102449
60	73,784	1,662	0.9774748	0.0225252
70	53,225	2,263	0.9574824	0.0425176
80	23,506	2,835	0.8793925	0.1206075
90	3,705	862	0.7673414	0.2326586
100	802	257	0.6795511	0.3204489

where,

X	age
l_x	The number of people who survive to age x – note that this is based on a starting point of l_0 lives, typically taken as 100,000, where $l_{x+1} = l_x(1 - q_x) = l_x p_x$, where $p_x = \dfrac{l_{x+1}}{l_x}$
d_x	the number of people who die aged x last birthday where $d_x = l_x - l_{x+1} = l_x(1 - p_x) = l_x q_x$
p_x	the probability that someone aged exactly x will survive to age $(x + 1)$. $p_x = 1 - q_x$
q_x	the probability that someone aged exactly x will die before reaching age $(x + 1)$
It is custom to denote	
w as	maximum age at which the table ends up (in case above $w = 100$)

Note that d_x and l_x are the values that are taken from the statistical observation and are usually provided by the statistical office, where the last variables are just a rearrangement.

On the basis of the mortality table, the following notation can be constructed:

$_n p_x$ the probability that someone aged exactly x will survive for n more years, that is, live up to at least age $x + n$ years.

$$_n P_x = \frac{l_{x+n}}{l_x} \tag{A1.15}$$

$_{m|n} q_x$ the probability that someone aged exactly x will survive for m more years, then die within the following n years.

$$_{m|n} q_x = {}_m P_x \times {}_n q_{x+m} = \frac{l_{x+m} - l_{x+m+n}}{l_x} \tag{A1.16}$$

A lifetime annuity is an annuity that ends at the death of the insured person.

Example:

Construct the value of the lifetime ordinary annuity of 1 euro.

Solution:

In this simple case, a given number of people, say l_x, want to pay an unknown amount into a bank account. This value should be enough to pay each of the l_x founders the life annuity of 1 euro each year until his/

her death. Let us denote the amount of money that should be contributed by each founder as a_x. The entire amount at the date of funding the capital will be $l_x a_x$. This amount of money will yield interest on the deposit at the rate i_a (actuarial technical rate of return). The initial $l_x a_x$ amount would be reduced by the subsequent payment of the annuities of 1 euro to the surviving founders. By introducing $v^x = (1 + i_a)^{-x}$, then:

$$l_x a_x = v^1 l_{x+1} + v^2 l_{x+2} + v^3 l_{x+3} + \ldots + v^{w-x-1} l_{w-1}$$

where $w-$ is the maximum age (say 100 years).

By dividing both sides by l_x and subsequently the right-hand side by v^x we arrive at:

$$a_x = \frac{(v^{x+1} \, l_{x+1} + \; v^{x+2} \, l_{x+2} + v^{x+3} \, l_{x+3} + \ldots. + v^{w-1} \, l_{w-1}}{v^x \, l_x}$$

This a_x represents the ordinary life annuity. A similar concept might be applied to the immediate life annuity.

a_x is actually discounted with two factors: first is the time value of money, and second is the probability of surviving for given periods. Thus, the difference between the financial instrument and the insurance contract lies with the application of a death probability as the discount factor.

There are two different rates used for the actuarial and financial instruments calculation. The actuarial rate is the insurance technical rate that roughly represents the return on the actuarial reserve placement, whereas in financial instruments, we usually refer to the money market rates (e.g., LIBOR) that are an approximation of the bank deposits rate. This observation provides the fundamental information for comparative studies of different insurance and investment products.

Analysis of bank deposit versus an endowment policy (a life insurance contract designed to pay a lump sum after a specified term (its maturity) or on death).

For simplicity, let us consider both a deposit and an endowment of 1 euro, thus:

The endowment for a person of x age for n ($_n E_x$) years is equal to:

$$_n E_x = v_{un}^n p_x \tag{A1.17}$$

where v_u^n is a discount factor based on the technical insurance rate i_a,

$$v_u^n = \frac{1}{\left(1+i_a\right)^n} \tag{A1.18}$$

while the bank deposit value is equal to:

$$PV = 1 v_b^n \tag{A1.19}$$

where v_b^n is a discount factor based on the bank deposit rate i_b,

$$v_b^n = \frac{1}{\left(1+i_b\right)^n} \tag{A1.20}$$

and since the endowment and bank deposit should be equal:

$$_n E_x = PV \tag{A1.21}$$

then:

$$v_b^n = v_{un}^n p_x \tag{A1.22}$$

thus:

$$\frac{1}{\left(1+i_b\right)^n} = \frac{1}{\left(1+i_a\right)^n} \, _n p_x \tag{A1.23}$$

By arranging the equation versus i_b

$$i_b = \left[\frac{1}{\left(1+i_a\right)^n} \times {}_n p_x \right]^{-\frac{1}{n}} - 1 \tag{A1.24}$$

The i_b is the lowest rate a bank must offer to be as competitive as the endowment issued by the insurer for a person at age x. This is true under the assumption of the net endowment calculation and for a bank rate given for a period of n years.

Let us consider the same issues for a loan. For example, a loan is drawn at a notional value of 10,000 euros with a nominal interest rate of 7%. The bank will usually calculate the fixed installments over the period of the loan, for example, 3 years.

First, the bank has to ascertain the value of the deposit required for an annuity with a PV of 10,000 euros at the rate of 7% for 3 years:

$$10,000 = \frac{X}{1.07^1} + \frac{X}{1.07^2} + \frac{X}{1.07^3} \text{ then } X\left(\frac{1}{1.07^1} + \frac{1}{1.07^2} + \frac{1}{1.07^3}\right) = 10,000$$

therefore, $X = 10,000\left(\frac{1}{1.07^1} + \frac{1}{1.07^2} + \frac{1}{1.07^3}\right)^{-1} = 3,810$

The 3-year installments of 3,810 at the rate of 7% p.a. is equivalent to a one-off payment of 10,000 euro. Using this information, let us look at the schedules:

	Balance	Interest at 7%	Payment	Balance Y/E	Capital repaid
1	10,000	700	3,810	6,890	3,110
2	6,890	482	3,810	3,562	3,328
3	3,562	249	3,812	0	3,563
	Total		11,430		10,000

Note that the last installment is a rounded figure.

The table above is called the loan amortization schedule.

There is a rule for the quick approximation of loan payments.

Suppose that i_m is the monthly interest rate (quick approximation monthly $\cong \dfrac{\text{yearly rate}}{12}$) on the loan of total value $L€$, taken for n months would be:

$$M = \frac{Li_m\left(1+i_m\right)^n}{\left(1+i_m\right)^n - 1} \tag{A1.25}$$

Example:

You are going to take a loan of value 10,000 for 3 years, at a yearly interest rate of 12%. What would be your monthly installment?

Solution:

$i_m = 12\%/12 = 1\%$, $n = 12 \times 3 = 36$, $L = 10{,}000$ then
$M = 10{,}000 \times 0.01 \times (1.01)^3 \times 12 / ((1 + 0.01)^{12} - 1) = 332$

Up to now, we have used either of the interest rates for our calculation. In practice, we differentiate between nominal and real interest rates. Nominal interest rate is the rate observed on the market, whereas real interest rate is the rate stripped of inflation. The link between nominal and real interest rates is:

$$1 + \text{real rate} = \frac{1 + \text{nominal rate}}{1 + \text{rate of inflation}} \tag{A1.26}$$

Thus

$$\text{real rate} = \frac{\text{nominal rate} - \text{rate of inflation}}{1 + \text{rate of inflation}} \tag{A1.27}$$

This equation holds true for compounded interest; it can be simplified for continuous interest:

Real rate of interest = nominal rate − inflation rate.

Therefore, it is easier to manipulate with rates with the continuous capitalization assumption.

Note that a frequent mistake when calculating the present and future values is the mismatch between the nominal rates and real cash flow (stripped of inflation), or nominal cash flow (including inflation effect) and a real rate.

Another assumption used until now was that the value of deposits (or money received) does not change. We are going to remove this assumption and consider a situation where different amounts are received or paid at different times.

Let us consider an example where we expect to receive 20 euros after 1 year, then we must pay 50 euros after 2 years, and finally we receive 300 euros at the end of year 3.

The cash flow from the above would look like this:

	After 1 Year	After 2 Years	After 3 Years
Cash flows	20	(50)	25
Values inside parenthesis indicate that they are negative.			

The number in brackets represents a negative value, meaning a cash outflow, whereas the positive number represents a cash inflow.

What would be the equivalent of this cash flow (net present value) paid in one lump sum now, when the market interest rate is 10%?

	After 1 Year	After 2 Years	After 3 Years
Cash flow	20	(50)	25
The discount is	$(1+10\%)^{-1}$	$(1+10\%)^{-2}$	$(1+10\%)^{-3}$
Discount value	0.91	0.83	0.75
Present value	18	(41)	19
Sum of present values −4			
Values inside parenthesis indicate that they are negative.			

The net present value (NPV) can be either negative or positive. It serves as a decision-making tool. A project with a negative NPV should not be undertaken as it generates a loss.

The NPV of the different cash flows can be analytically stated as:

$$\text{NPV} = \sum_{t=0}^{n} \frac{C_t}{(1+i)^t} \tag{A1.28}$$

where C_t is the cash flow at the year t,

Whereas the future value would be:

$$\text{FV} = \sum_{t=0}^{n} C_t (1+i)^{n-t} \tag{A1.29}$$

Note: If it is the case that cash flow is denominated in a foreign currency, then the interest rate must be denominated in the same currency.

When calculating, we sometimes ask ourselves the question: at what rate would the NPV be equal to zero? This is called the internal rate of return (IRR).

Let us continue the example above and calculate the internal rate of return as a trial and error exercise.

Rate	69%		
	After 1 Year	After 2 Years	After 3 Years
Cash flows	20	(50)	25
The discount is	0.59	0.35	0.21
Present value	12	(18)	5
NPV	0		
Values inside parenthesis indicate that they are negative.			

The IRR is equal to 69% for this project. The IRR is used as the decision parameter when the required return rate is known or for a comparison between two or more projects.

The IRR can be found by linear approximation. Assuming that we found negative and positive NPVs at different discount rates, then:

$$IRR_{app} = i_1 + \frac{NPV_1}{NPV_1 + |NPV_2|} \times (i_2 - i_1) \qquad (A1.30)$$

where,

IRR_{app} = approximation of internal rates of return,
NPV_1 = NPV at i_1
NPV_2 = NPV at i_2
i_1 = rate at positive value of NPV, and
i_2 = rate at negative value of NPV.

To illustrate the formula, consider the following graph:

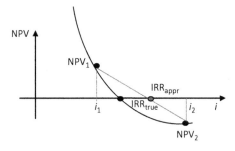

where IRR_{true} represents the IRR rate.

The reasoning for a graphical approximation of IRR is that for IRR_{appr} the closer the i_1 and i_2 are to each other, the closer IRR_{appr} is to IRR_{true}.

For specific cash flows, there is no real solution for IRR.

Consider the following example:

An investment of 100 euros now brings the following cash flows: 200 euros at the end of year 1, and a 101 euro cash outflow at the end of year 2. As a result of this, the equation is:

$$-100 + 200/(1+i) - 101/(1+i)^2 = 0$$

There is no real number solution (only complex roots).

There could be more than one solution to IRR.

Consider the following scenario: a project is earning (190,000 euros), + 45,500 euros, 270,000 euros. In this case, there are two IRR solutions: 8.49% and 31%. There is "a rule of signs," that states that there can be as many positive solutions of IRR as there are changes of sign in the cash flow.

The decisions taken on NPV and IRR may in some circumstances be contradictory.

The NPV and IRR methods for project evaluation lead to conflicting results if:

The pattern of cash inflows plays an important role in project evaluation when using the IRR method; that is, the cash flows of one project may increase over time, whereas those of other projects may decrease, and vice versa. The major drawback with the IRR method is that for mutually exclusive projects, it can give rise to contradictory investment decisions when compared with the NPV method.

Consider the following example:

Year	Project A (In Euros)	Project B (In Euros)
0	(1,000)	(1,000)
1	75	600
2	275	575
3	450	75
4	500	0
5	525	0
IRR	19%	15%
NPV	198 euros	250 euros
Values inside parenthesis indicate that they are negative.		

In the above example, A and B are mutually exclusive projects. Both projects require an initial outlay of 1,000 euros, but the pattern of cash inflows is different. Cash inflows for Project A are increasing over the period of time while those for Project B are decreasing over time. A decision based on the IRR method would lead us to select Project A over Project B as the IRR of Project A is greater than the IRR of Project B. A decision based on a calculation of NPV would imply that project B is more valuable. If the company was to select a project based solely on IRR, a less profitable project would be chosen.

Graphical summary of typical cash flow patterns.

Graphic Representation	Instrument Type
Graphic representation	One-off investment – initial cash outflow is usually smaller than the subsequent cash inflow
	Ordinary annuity – a fixed amount is invested regularly at given intervals. At the end of the investment period, a lump sum is paid
	Ordinary annuity – a lump sum is invested at the initial date, and subsequently, a fixed amount of cash is paid at equal intervals

Graphic Representation	Instrument Type
	Annuity – a fixed amount is invested at equal intervals, starting with an initial investment, and after the investment period, a fixed amount is received as a lump sum
	Annuity due – a lump sum is invested at the beginning of the investment period, and from the beginning of the investment period, a fixed installment is received at fixed intervals
	Perpetuity due – a lump sum is paid immediately and a fixed amount is received immediately, followed by payments at fixed intervals indefinitely
	Ordinary perpetuity due – a lump sum is paid, and a fixed amount is paid after the first interval and subsequently at fixed intervals indefinitely
	Nonregular cash flow in regular time slots

Altman, E.I., 1968. Financial Ratios, Discriminant Analysis and the Prediction of Corporate Bankruptcy. Journal of Finance 23 (4), 589–609.

Akerlof, G., 1970. The Market for "Lemons": Quality Uncertainty and the Market Mechanism. The Quarterly Journal of Economics 84 (3), 488–500.

Bhole, L.M., 2004. Financial Institutions and Markets: Structure, Growth and Innovations, 4e Tata McGraw-Hill Education, New Delhi.

Bodie, Z., Merton, R.C., Cleeton, D., 2009. Financial Economics. Pearson Learning Solutions Upper Saddle River, Pearson/Prentice Hall.

Cole, V., Branson, J., Breesch, D., 2011. The Illusion of Comparable European IFRS Financial Statements. Beliefs of Auditors and Other Users. Accounting & Management Information Systems / Contabilitate si Informatica de Gestiune 10 (2), 106–134.

Cukierman, A., 1992. Central Bank Strategy, Credibility, and Independence: Theory and Evidence. MIT Press, USA.

Chandavarkar, A.G., 1992. Central Banking in Developing Countries. Macmillan Press, Houndmills, Basingstoke, Hampshire; St. Martin's Press, New York.

Davis, M., Kumiega, A., Van Vliet, B., 2013. Ethics, Finance, and Automation: A Preliminary Survey of Problems in High Frequency Trading. Science and Engineering Ethics 19 (3), 851–874.

Divis, K., Teply, P., 2005. Information efficiency of Central Europe stock exchanges. Finance a Uver-Czech Journal of Economics and Finance 55 (9–10), 471–482.

Fabozzi, F.J., 2003. The Handbook of Financial Instruments. John Wiley & Sons, Hoboken, New Jersey.

Fama, E.F., 1970. Efficient Capital Markets: A Review of Theory and Empirical Work. The Journal of Finance 25 (2), 383–417.

Flannery, M.J., 2010. Stabilizing Large Financial Institutions with Contingent Capital Certificates.

Grossman, S.J., Stiglitz, J.E., 1980. On the Impossibility of Informationally Efficient Markets. The American Economic Review 70 (3), 393–408.

Greenbaum, S.I., Thakor, A.V., 2007. Contemporary Financial Intermediation. Academic Press, Burlington, San Diego, London.

Fama, E.F., French, K.R., 1993. Common Risk Factors in the Returns on Stocks and Bonds. Journal of Financial Economics 33 (1), 3–56.

Hartmann, P., Manna, M., Manzanares, A., 2001. The Microstructure of the Euro Money Market. Journal of International Money and Finance 20 (6), 895–948.

Hull, J., 2005. Fundamentals Of Futures And Options Markets. Pearson/Prentice Hall, Upper Saddle River, New Jersey.

Klingebiel, D., Cleasssens, S., 2001. Competition and Scope of Activities in Financial Services. World Bank Research Observer 16 (1), 19–40.

Knight, F., 1921. Risk, Uncertainty and Profit, 1971st ed. The University Chicago Press, Chicago.

Le, T.T.T., Ooi, J.T.L., 2012. Financial Structure of Property Companies and Capital Market Development. Journal of Property Investment & Finance 30 (6), 596–611.

Finance: A Quantitative Introduction. http://dx.doi.org/10.1016/B978-0-12-801584-1.00020-2

Mandel, B., Morgan, D., Wei, C., 2012. The Role of Bank Credit Enhancements in Securitization. New York Economic Policy Review, New York.

Miller, M., 1999. The History of Finance. The Journal of Portfolio Management, 95–101.

Power, M., 2004. The Risk Management of Everything. Journal of Risk Finance 5 (3), 58–65.

Stiglitz, J., 1975. The Theory of "Screening," Education, and the Distribution of Income. The American Economic Review 65 (3), 238–300.

Statman, M., 1995. Behavioral Finance versus Standard Finance. AIMR Conference Proceedings. pp. 14–25.

Taylor, J.B., Williams, J.C., 2009. A Black Swan in the Money Market. American Economic Journal: Macroeconomics 1 (1), 58–83.

Printed in the United States
By Bookmasters